
Theresa Youssef's Vegetable Gardening for Beginners

ALSO BY WASFI YOUSSEF

1. All You Need to Know Before Buying a Home
2. Building Your Own Home

Praise for *All You Need to Know Before Buying a Home*

"Must read. This guide to home buying really lives up to its title.... This detail-oriented book is ideal for home buyers who want to carefully research before searching for a home. After studying this book, the reader will know more about buying a home than virtually any real estate agent. "
—Chicago Tribune

"All that buyers need to know, in plain words.... This book stands out in its nine chapters on inspection, covering every part of the house from the neighborhood to the yard, from the kitchen to the basement and from the utilities to the radon. After a close reading of the inspection section, a house hunter could give a home a pretty thorough looking over, even without hiring a professional inspector. "
—Gannett Suburban Newspapers

List Price: $19.95*

Published and distributed by: Alpha Publishing
4 Carol Lane
Mamaroneck, New York 10543
Tel/Fax: (914) 381-5377

Praise for *Building Your Own Home*

"Building Your Own Home is an encyclopedia reference guide.... It's a superb reference guide.... Chapters 2 through 18 focus on the steps one must take before construction.... The next 24 chapters of the book deal with major phases of construction."

—The Boston Sunday Globe

"This book should prove profitable reading for prospective home builders and remodelers as well as appraisers, architects, real estate agents, and developers. It is well organized and complete, a virtual bible of necessary knowledge for anyone involved in home building."
**—San Francisco Sunday
Examiner and Chronicle**

List Price: 27.95*

Published by John Wiley & Sons, Inc.

---

* Price may change without prior notice.

Theresa Youssef's Vegetable Gardening for Beginners

Theresa Youssef
Wasfi Youssef

Alpha Publishing

Mamaroneck, New York 10543

Published and Distributed by: Alpha Publishing
4 Carol Lane
Mamaroneck, N.Y. 10543
Tel/Fax: (914) 381-5377

Editor, Cover Photo, and Book Design: Wasfi Youssef
Copy Editing: Suzanne B. Davidson
Typesetting and Production: Alpha Publishing

Library of Congress Catalog Card No: 00-091007

ISBN 0-9632423-2-6

Printed in the United States of America

To the Memory of Theresa's Beloved Father JOSEPH MISTIKAWI and Beloved Brother FOUAD MISTIKAWI who loved life and spent countless hours gardening and enjoying nature in all its beauty and wonder. We tender our love and gratitude to both.

Preface

The idea to write this book was inspired by a course in speech Theresa took some years ago at Baruch College in midtown Manhattan. The instructor for that course was Professor R. Stearns. One of the course's requirements was for Theresa to deliver a speech to persuade her classmates to do something. Because gardening was, and still is, Theresa's favorite hobby, she chose to persuade her classmates to grow their own vegetables.

The presentation was a great success. When Theresa finished the speech, her classmates gave her a strong round of applause. More importantly, Professor Stearns, who is a gardener herself, congratulated her. After Theresa made the presentation, Professor Stearns asked the class, "Did Theresa convince you to grow your own vegetables?" The response was a loud "yes." The professor affirmed that by saying, "she darned did."

In her comments on the written report that Theresa submitted as a part of the course's requirements, Professor Stearns wrote,

> A well organized and beautifully <u>supported</u> ('facts & figures,' personal narrative, visual aid) speech w/improved direct person-to-person—and at the end you even seemed to be <u>enjoying it.</u> Keep it up!

The underlines and punctuations are the professor's. Well, Theresa kept it it up by co-writing this book!

The cover photo of this book was one of two photos that Theresa showed her classmates as a part of her presentation. The photo was kept in an album that no one had seen for years. Theresa wasn't even aware of its existence until she looked for some photos to support her presentation. We thought the picture was beautiful. We framed and hung it in our kitchen. When Theresa thought of writing this book, we both decided to use the photo for the cover of the book.

Theresa inherited the love for gardening from her grandfather and father (to whose memory this book is dedicated). Her grandfather, who lived in an apartment, used to grow tomatoes in pots on his balcony. Even though Theresa was a little child then, she still remembers how excited she was to watch grandpa's tomatoes grow and how good they tasted. During the growing season, she couldn't wait to visit her grandpa, or rather his tomatoes, in order to pick and eat the ripe ones.

Years later, when Theresa's father retired, he started a vegetable garden. The plot was small, but Father managed to plant several vegetables. A tour in the garden was a must for his close friends! Gardening kept him active and happy. The other family members were no less happy. Whenever Mother needed some vegetables from the garden, everyone competed to pick them for her!

Then we got married. We lived in a third-floor apartment in Flushing, New York. The apartment had a balcony facing east and received direct sun from early morning to early afternoon. Both of us gardened. We grew several vegetables and herbs in pots. The most rewarding crop by far was tomatoes. We grew them in 10-inch pots. During the harvest season, big tomato fruits could be seen through the balcony's railing by passersby and neighbors. In some years, the harvest was so big that we gave some to our friends. Many of our neighbors complimented us for our success and wondered how tomatoes could grow so big in pots. They wanted to know the secret of our success!

Several years later, we moved to a detached house. As expected, we started a garden the same year. The plot was rocky and bare. We had to import subsoil and topsoil. It was costly, but we enjoy gardening so much. To us, it is a lot of fun. During the season, our guests ask us to show them the garden, and we happily oblige. You can see the excitement on their faces when they see the plants bearing fruit. When the time of eating comes, we proudly mention which vegetables are from the garden: the lettuce, tomatoes, cucumbers, and parsley in the salad; the eggplants in *baba ghannouj* (the recipe is given in chapter 26); the potatoes in the lamb stew; and so on.

When our guests are ready to leave, we give them some produce. Sometimes, they like to pick what they want themselves. It is more fun this way. It is very rewarding when some of the guests call us later to say how tasty and fresh our produce is.

Several of our brothers, sisters, and in-laws love gardening. They live in different parts of the country, Theresa's sister lived for 18 years in Tennessee, her brother lived in Massachusetts, Wasfi's brother lives in Northern California, and we live in Westchester County, about 30 miles north of New York City. We talk often with our gardening relatives and share our experience. This gives us a good perspective about the effect of geographic location on gardening. For example, in Tennessee they grow okra with relative ease because the weather is hot, while in our area, it is difficult because the weather is cool. We incorporated this knowledge into the book.

Some of the photos in the book show brand name products. We also give the names of some seed catalogs. These should not be taken as an endorsement for these products and seed catalogs.

With some effort and a little bit of luck, you too will have an enjoyable and rewarding gardening experience.

Contents

Part 5   Very-Tender Vegetables   197

Introduction

Every year, millions of men and women of all ages become interested in growing their own vegetables. They buy several seed packets or a few packs of seedlings and put them in the ground without giving any thought to what the seeds and seedlings need to grow or under what conditions each vegetable plant grows healthy and bears fruit. In many cases, the seeds germinate poorly (or don't germinate at all) and the seedlings grow weak and produce a few small fruits. They throw in the towel and give up. They think that growing vegetables is difficult and that they are not cut out to be vegetable growers.

Fortunately, these individuals can grow vegetables like a pro if they know the basic information concerning gardening and the characteristics of each vegetable plant. This book explains this information in simple terms that a layman can understand. It is divided into 6 parts.

Part 1, entitled "Basics," explains the basic information you need to know about vegetable gardening. It is divided into 9 chapters.

Chapter 1, entitled "The Benefits of Gardening," explains that gardening is not only a source of fresh, tasty, and nutritious vegetables and herbs, but also a therapy for the body and soul. Gardening activity is good physical exercise. The garden is a place where you can relax after a day full of hard work. It is where the family get together to enjoy, learn, explore, and have fun. It keeps youngsters occupied and out of trouble and is a pastime for seniors.

Growing your vegetables and herbs successfully saves money. In addition to the price of vegetables, gardening saves car mileage by cutting down on the trips you need to make to buy vegetables and herbs. The saving can be significant if you have a big family to feed and a big garden.

Chapter 2, "Essentials of Successful Gardening," explains the information you need to know to be a successful gardener. After a close reading of this chapter, you will know more about growing vegetables and herbs than many who have been gardening for years. This chapter includes 19 topics. They include how to choose a good site, what makes good soil, organic material, the temperatures within which each vegetable plant grows well, the pH value of the soil, and a comprehensive description of fertilizers, including how to read the labels, which brands are good, and what kind to apply to each plant.

In this chapter, we introduce what we call *Theresa's Alternative Method.* It is a simple and easy way of preparing the soil for vegetable gardening. In this method, there is no need to till the entire area or have the whole garden covered with topsoil. Rather, the vegetables and herbs are planted in holes and trenches dug in the garden and filled with potting soil. The dimensions of the holes and trenches, the spacings between them, and the composition of the potting soil for each vegetable are given in the pertinent chapter. We have been using this method for several years with great success. It saves us a considerable amount of effort.

Chapter 3 explains how to plan for your garden. The minimum space each vegetable plant needs and the yield per plant are given. An important aspect of planning is vegetable hardiness—the ability of the vegetable plant to tolerate cold weather. We divided the vegetables into 4 categories: very-hardy, hardy, tender, and very-tender. The vegetable plants should be planted in the sequence of their hardiness. Also explained in this chapter is how to plant more than one crop in one season even if you live in cool areas like the northern United States.

Chapter 4 explains the factors you should consider when deciding whether to grow vegetables from seeds or seedlings. The main factors are the climate where you live and the hardiness of each vegetable. Also explained are the best and cheapest way to buy seeds and seedlings. Leftover seeds can be used in the following years. The number of years each vegetable seed can be used is given.

Chapter 5 explains organic gardening. It is a method of growing vegetables and herbs without the use of chemical fertilizers and pesticides. Plant nutrients are provided by organic material. Harmful insects and diseases are managed by nontoxic means. The most widely used organic materials and their characteristics are given in this chapter. We also explain composting, the process whereby the organic material is converted into fertilizers the plants can absorb and a soil conditioner. Since this book is not about organic gardening, we give the reader the titles of several books about the subject and the address of Rodale Press, which is the leader in publishing books about organic gardening.

For all practical purposes, we consider ourselves to be organic gardeners. This is because we rarely use pesticides. The only difference is that organic gardeners fertilize their vegetables exclusively with organic material, especially manure, while we use a mixture of chemical fertilizers and organic material. All the literature we read indicates that the plants don't distinguish between organic and commercial fertilizers.

Chapter 6 explains the benefits of earthworms and how to increase their number in your garden. Suffice it to say that earthworms' castings contain 5 times more soluble nitrogen, 7 times more phosphorous, 3 times more magnesium, and 1.5 times more calcium than is contained in the food the worms eat.

Chapter 7 explains how to grow vegetables and herbs in containers. Our definition of a container is anything that can hold moist soil and has a drainage hole at its bottom, including pots. The tools for growing vegetables and herbs in containers successfully are the right-size container for each vegetable or herb, good potting soil, adequate fertilizing, frequent watering, and weeding. Of course, the site should have at least 8 hours of direct sunlight daily.

Chapter 8 discusses two major vegetable garden pests, animals and harmful insects. Animal pests are something you have to contend with in the course of gardening. They include woodchucks, rabbits, rats, mice, chipmunks, squirrels, deer, skunks, and raccoons. These animals' habitat, food preferences, and what you can do to fend them off are given in this chapter. Also in this chapter we explain briefly some of the harmful insects, the damage they may inflict on vegetable plants, and how to control them. A colored illustration of many harmful insects and the pesticide that kills each can be found in a chart produced by the Ortho Company. You may be able to get a free copy of this chart from a nearby big nursery.

In chapter 9 we discuss the contribution of home-grown vegetables to good health. Home-grown vegetables and herbs are rich in vitamins, minerals, and fiber, which are essential to good health and a strong immune system. This is because you pick the vegetables at the peak of ripeness and because you don't spray them with any pesticides unless absolutely necessary. We explain the role each vitamin, mineral, and fiber plays in good health, the ill effects of its deficiency, and the vegetables and herbs that contain it.

The following 22 chapters describe how to grow 18 vegetables and 4 herbs. For consistency, the information is organized in the same order for all the vegetables. They include an opening statement, time to plant, general information, preparing the soil for planting according to the conventional method and Theresa's alternative method, planting, caring for, harvesting, diseases, insects, varieties (please note that seed growers continually develop new varieties, while dropping unpopular ones), and nutritive value. For the herbs, we deviated a little from this sequence. We omitted some topics that we thought were irrelevant and added medicinal benefits, where applicable.

For simplicity and clarity we made the text concise and relied more on photos. Realizing that not every gardener will plant all the vegetables and herbs included in the book, we made every chapter independent of the others.

The 18 vegetables are grouped in 4 parts according to their hardiness and the 4 herbs are grouped in another part.

Part 2 is about very-hardy vegetables. Very-hardy vegetables are the first to be planted in the season. They take overnight temperatures as low as 21º F (-6.1º C). You can plant them outdoors 4 to 6 weeks before the last spring frost. The vegetables included in this part are onions, lettuce, spinach, peas, cabbage, potatoes, and broccoli.

Part 3 is about hardy vegetables. Hardy vegetables take overnight temperatures as low as 27º F (-2.8º C). They can be planted outdoors 3 to 4 weeks before the last frost. The vegetables included in this part are beets, carrots, and radishes.

Part 4 is about tender vegetables. Tender vegetables cannot take temperatures below 40º F (4.4º C). Therefore, they must be planted after the danger of frost is gone. If the temperature falls below 40º F, the plants should be either covered or brought indoors. The vegetables included in this part are tomatoes, summer squashes, sweet corn, and beans.

Part 5 is about very-tender vegetables. Very-tender vegetables cannot take temperatures below 50º F (10º C). They should be planted outdoors 3 weeks after the last frost. Very-tender vegetables included in this part are peppers, cucumbers, eggplants, and okra.

Part 6 is about herbs. Herbs may be perennial or annual. Perennial herbs are very hardy. Annual herbs may be hardy or tender. Herbs included in this part are parsley (annual, hardy), mint (perennial, very-hardy), basil (annual, tender), and catnip (perennial, very-hardy).

Consistent with our goal of enjoying eating the vegetables and herbs we grow, we present several simple recipes for healthy meals that include home-grown vegetables and herbs.

A last word about measurement systems. We in the United States still use the foot to measure lengths and the degree Fahrenheit to measure temperatures, while practically the rest of the world use the meter to measure lengths and the degree centigrade to measure temperatures. To make it easy for the reader, we include the measurement values in both systems.

Part 1

Basics

Chapters in This Part

Chapter 1

The Benefits of Gardening

Gardening is a great hobby. Whether you live in a detached house, townhouse (row house), condominium, cooperative, or apartment with a sunny balcony, you can enjoy growing vegetables and herbs. You may be single, married, divorced, or separated and still enjoy this great hobby. Age is no barrier. Children as well as seniors can practice gardening without difficulty. And there are many benefits to growing your own vegetables.

Fresh and Tasty Vegetables

There is no comparison between the freshness, taste, flavor, and nutritive value of the vegetables you grow in your garden and those you buy in the market. When you grow your vegetables, you pick them at the peak of ripeness, then wash and eat them raw or cooked shortly thereafter. This way, their vitamins and nutritive value are not diminished. By contrast, the vegetables sold in the market are picked days and sometimes weeks before they reach the stores. Then they stay on the shelves for several more days. By the time you buy them, a considerable amount of their flavor and vitamins is lost.

One of the pleasures of gardening is the quality of the produce. One vegetable that we enjoy eating early in the season is snow peas. We love Chinese cooking, for which snow peas are a basic ingredient. However, we find the snow peas sold in the market to be of inferior quality, even though they are expensive. Therefore, we decided to grow our own and we find the difference in taste and flavor remarkable.

The same can be said about the quality of the cucumbers that are sold in the market. Although inexpensive, they taste awful! This is because they are waxed in order to prevent rot while they are on the shelves for a long time. By contrast, the burpless cucumber variety that we grow is so tasty and easy to digest that we eat them with the skin. You cannot buy this variety from the market at any price.

With increasing health awareness, it is important to know that the vegetables you grow at home are practically organic. This is because you don't need to use herbicides (weed killers) and rarely use insecticides and fungicides. All the pesticides in the vegetables we eat accumulate in our bodies and weaken our immune systems, the main defense against diseases.

An Educational and Exciting Experience

Watching vegetables grow from tiny seeds or seedlings to big plants that bear fruit is both educational and exciting. Each day brings something new: the seeds germinate, true leaves appear, flowers bloom and are pollinated by the bees, the pollinated flowers become fruits, and so on. As the vegetables grow, your mouth waters each time you walk into the garden. You wait impatiently for the day when they ripen. As soon as they do, picking and eating them fresh is great fun. The first vegetable you pick and eat is the tastiest.

One of the learning experiences of gardening is the ability to identify each plant while it is still tiny. Most people who don't garden cannot distinguish one plant from another until they bear fruit.

Watching the plants grow and bear fruit makes you aware of the miracle that creates life. It is amazing how one tiny seed grows into a huge tomato plant while another tiny seed grows to become a lettuce or eggplant. Early in our gardening experience, we wondered how the beefsteak tomato vine could support a cluster of 3 huge fruits. We expected it to break. To our amazement, it did not!

Many vegetable plants produce beautiful flowers. This is to attract the bees

One of the learning experiences of gardening is the ability to identify each plant while it is still tiny: top left is zucchini, top right is pepper.

that pollinate them and make them reproduce. A spectacular bouquet emerges when the zucchini plants flower. One morning you wake up to see huge yellow flowers that have bloomed overnight. They rival the petunias! When the early flowers fall off without bearing fruit, you become con-

A spectacular bouquet emerges when the zucchini plants flower.

cerned. You think that something is wrong with the zucchini. Then you learn that the first zucchini flowers are males. Their function is to pollinate the female flowers, which appear about 10 days later. With good observation, you will be able to differentiate between male and female zucchini stems. The male's stem is slim, while the female's stem is thick and looks like a tiny zucchini. When pollinated, the stem grows into a full fruit within a few days. The same is true for cucumbers, although their flowers are much smaller than those of zucchini.

With good observation, you will be able to differentiate between male (far left) and female (left) zucchini stems.

Promoting Social Behavior

Gardening makes neighbors talk to each other. Usually, people position their vegetable garden along the border of their property. Each neighbor can see his or her neighbors' gardens. This gives them the opportunity to chat with each other. Everyone is curious to know what the neighbors are planting, which vegetables grow best and which grow poorly, whether the neighbors grow from seeds or seedlings, where they buy seeds and seedlings, and what kind of fertilizers they use. We hardly see our neighbors during winter. It is as if we hibernate! But when the gardening season begins, we see and talk to each other frequently. We exchange not only information, but also produce. Often one neighbor grows too much of one vegetable while another grows too much of another. They usually exchange crops, each one trying to be more generous than the other!

Office employees love to talk about their gardens during coffee breaks. It makes a nice piece of conversation. Sometimes those who garden bring some of their vegetables for colleagues who don't have gardens. Soon it becomes a sort of competition for who has the biggest and tastiest vegetables.

We grow a lot of vegetables in containers in front of our garage door. Early in the season, when the plants are still tiny seedlings, neighbors stop by and ask what are we growing. They show great interest in learning which seedlings are what. When the plants grow and bear fruit, they stop by and wonder how zucchini, tomatoes, and cucumbers can grow in pots. When one of us picks and hands them some vegetables, their faces brighten!

During one growing season, a man from the telephone company came to repair our telephone line. When he saw the numerous fruit-bearing vegetables grown in containers, he stopped to look. He couldn't believe he was seeing the cucumbers, zucchini, beans, and more, all bearing fruit. Wasfi offered him a bag full of cucumbers, which he gratefully accepted. He took them to his truck and, forgetting what he came for, started the engine. Then he realized that he had not fixed our telephone. He stopped the engine and came back, apologizing!

Good Physical Exercise

Gardening is good physical exercise. Tilling, planting, weeding, watering, harvesting, and so on require the movement of many of your body's muscles. These activities are performed outdoors in fresh air and at your own pace. There is no need for a videocassette instructing you how to move! Each day you do something different, which takes boredom out of physical exercise. We have a stationary bike, but rarely use it. After a few minutes of stationary riding, we become bored!

Gardening is also a good way to lose weight. We each lose a few pounds during the gardening season, which we attribute to two factors: (1) exercising in the open, and (2) eating a considerable amount of fresh vegetables, which reduces our meat consumption. Eating more vegetables and less meat lowers cholesterol and reduces numerous ailments.

Keeping Youngsters Occupied and Out of Trouble

Youngsters have a lot of energy. If their energy is not channeled into something useful and benign, they can turn to destructive habits: smoking, drugs, alcohol, and other harmful and dangerous activities. Getting them interested at an early age in gardening absorbs a lot of their energy and directs it into something useful. When they learn how to plant and care for vegetables and see them grow, they turn away from bad thoughts. And when they eat something they grew, they get a feeling of accomplishment and satisfaction.

Getting youngsters interested in gardening at an early age absorbs a lot of their energy and directs it into something useful.

Pastime for Senior Citizens

Senior citizens who retire or become widows or widowers need something to keep them busy and active. Some of them cannot do much physical activity, but their minds are alert and sharp. Gardening is an excellent pastime for them. If they have enough energy and strength, they can grow vegetables in a garden. If they do not have the energy but have the means, they can hire someone to do the heavy work, such as tilling. If they have neither the energy nor the money, they can plant a small garden or grow vegetables and herbs in containers. Growing a few plants can give a lot of satisfaction to seniors.

Growing a few plants can give a lot of satisfaction to seniors.

A Place to Relax and Communicate with Nature

The vegetable garden is a place where you can relax after a long day full of problems and tension. As soon as you arrive home, you will find it irresistible to tour your garden before doing anything else. Once there, you will be at peace with yourself. Your mind will be clear. You will see the problems of life from a different perspective. You may be able to find solutions that you never thought of before for your problems. This is all done in harmony with nature and without the need for alcohol or drugs.

Once in the garden, you will be anxious to see new developments. The zucchini, cucumbers, and okra that were small yesterday are ready to be picked today. The tomatoes that were partially ripe the day before have ripened and are ready to be washed and eaten. The golden wax beans are dangling and waiting to be picked. You will have a great feeling of satisfaction and accomplishment when you return home carrying the day's harvest. At the dining table, family members will compliment each other on their success and accomplishment.

It is gratifying to know that your garden provides food for migrating birds and other wildlife. The robins arrive in early spring, and we are delighted to see them hopping about. Soon after their arrival, they build nests and lay eggs. They feed on earthworms and insects they find abundant in the garden. Often, a nest is built in a nearby tree, and we can see them feeding their young. Robins are dedicated parents. The male and female alternate guarding the nest and bringing worms to their always-hungry offspring. We can tell the males from the females by their color; the males have a darker brown breast than the females. Robins return each year to live and breed in the same spot where they hatched. In this respect, they are like salmon.

Other pleasant residents are the mockingbirds. They arrive in early to mid spring and fill the air with their lovely singing, switching from one tune to another so you sometimes don't know they are coming from the same bird. The singing starts early in the morning, shortly before first light, as if to announce that a new day is about to begin. In the afternoon, they stand on a high spot—the edge of the roof, a high tree branch, or a chimney—and sing their heart out. Sometimes, while relaxing on our deck, we think that they are singing for us!

Mockingbirds have a reputation of attacking much bigger birds that come close to their nest. We often see them chasing the much bigger crows. They even attack humans who come too close to their young! One year a pair of mockingbirds nested in a low hedge at the edge of our garden. This was a prime location because it was close to a good source of food. Whenever one of us stepped into the garden, one of the parents stood guard ready to attack us. Knowing their reputation, we kept our distance!

One year, a baby rabbit burrowed in our garden. Whenever one of us approached the garden, he (or she) would come out to greet us. While welcoming us, he would munch on the tender bean leaves. That would kill the bean plants, but we forgave him. When we entered the garden, he (or she) followed us! He was so cute that Wasfi took several pictures of him and kept them in an album. He loves to show the photos to our guests!

One year, a baby rabbit burrowed in our garden. Whenever one of us approached the garden, he (or she) would come out to greet us.

Fun

Gardening can be as much fun as you want it to be. We like to grow some vegetables in unconventional spots and containers. We have two small spots, each a few square feet, close to the side door. One year we decided to grow cucumbers in these spots. We thought it was cute to grow cucumbers as close as possible to the door. This way we didn't have to walk too far to pick cucumbers. When the plants grew, we trained them on the doorstep and throughout the season they kept producing. Imagine how much fun it was to have fresh cucumbers delivered to our doorstep.

Imagine how much fun it was to have fresh cucumbers delivered to our doorstep.

Saving Money

Gardening can save you money. Once your garden is established, it costs little to grow vegetables, particularly if you grow from seeds. The price of seedlings is small, particularly if you grow prolific vegetables such as zucchini and tomatoes. Other costs are the price of fertilizers, organic material, and water. Putting all the expenses together, we calculate that one lettuce costs as little as one penny, a pound of zucchini about 5 cents, and a pound of tomatoes about 10 cents. If you have a big family, a big garden can save you a considerable amount of money.

In addition to the price of vegetables, gardening saves car mileage by cutting down on the trips you need to make to buy vegetables. Every mile you drive to the market to buy vegetables, be they lettuce, parsley, tomatoes, or zucchini, costs gas and wear and tear on your car. This can become significant if the vegetable market is far from home.

Chapter 2

Essentials of Successful Gardening

The essence of successful vegetable gardening is to eat the fruits of your labor, literally speaking. If your plants don't grow and bear fruit that you and your family enjoy eating, you are not a successful gardener. Many beginners start by sowing some seeds or putting some seedlings in the ground thinking that they will automatically grow and bear fruit. They don't give any thoughts to the quality of the soil or the weather conditions each plant needs to grow and produce. In many cases the seeds don't germinate and the seedlings grow poorly and bear little or no fruit. Many of our friends who tried unsuccessfully to grow vegetables tell us that they sowed several packets of seeds in the ground but nothing came out, or that they planted several seedlings but got only one tomato or 2 peppers! They become frustrated and give up, thinking that vegetable gardening is not for them.

Fortunately, these individuals can garden like pros and enjoy a big harvest of tasty, fresh, and nutritious vegetables throughout the season if they know the essentials of successful gardening. The most important essentials are good site, good soil, organic material, humus, peat moss, mulch, proper temperature, proper pH value, water, fertilizers, pesticides, perlite and vermiculite, potting soil, planting methods, crop rotation, gardening tools, proper clothing, and continuous attention.

Good Site

A good site is one that gets direct sunlight all or most of the day. Sun provides the energy the plants need to grow. Ideally, sunlight must not be obstructed at any time of the day. However, this is not always possible. Your property may be small or for some other reason your garden needs to be close to the house or a big tree that you don't want to cut down. If this is the case, choose a location south of the high objects if you live in the Northern Hemisphere. (Conversely, choose a location north of the high objects if you live in the Southern Hemisphere, such as in Australia, South Africa, and South America.) This way, high objects will not obstruct direct sunlight to any part of the garden at any time of the day.

If the site you choose for your garden is east or west of nearby high objects, you still can grow vegetables successfully. Observe which areas get more sun and which areas get less sun throughout the day. The shade of high objects shifts continuously during the day, because of the rotation of the earth. Plant the fruit-bearing vegetables such as tomatoes, peppers, and eggplants in the areas that get at least 8 hours of direct sunlight daily. Plant leafy vegetables such as lettuce and spinach in the areas that get at least 6 hours of direct sunlight per day. And plant root crops such as potatoes, beets, and carrots in areas that get at least 7 hours of direct sunlight per day.

Also, place your garden at a respectable distance from big trees. In addition to obstructing direct sunlight, big trees deprive nearby vegetable plants of water and nutrients. This is because tree roots are very big compared to vegetable plant roots and, therefore, have more capacity to absorb the soil's nutrients and water.

If you cannot locate your garden far from big trees, give the area that lies on top of tree roots extra fertilizers and water and raise the level of the ground over the tree roots by adding topsoil. This added soil will provide the vegetable plant roots with a growing depth free of tree roots. If the trees are of the kind that develop shallow roots, like the maple and cottonwood, you will have to add more topsoil every couple of years.

For convenience and aesthetics, most people position their garden in the backyard. In houses having a small backyard, the garden may be positioned in the front.

In houses having a small backyard, the garden may be positioned in the front.

The surface of the ground should be flat or have a gentle slope. A gentle slope facing south (if you live in the Northern Hemisphere) increases the intensity of sunlight. This is desirable for tender and very-tender vegetables because they thrive on hot weather, and a gentle slope facing north (if you live in the Northern Hemisphere) reduces the intensity of sunlight. This is desirable for very-hardy and hardy vegetables, because they thrive on cool weather. If the surface is too steep, water from rain and irrigation will run off quickly instead of seeping through the soil. Moreover, heavy rain will wash away the topsoil and the valuable nutrients it contains. To absorb more rain and reduce soil wash, plant the rows across the slope.

If your area is windy, you may have to plant some high shrubs around the garden. The shrubs should be at least 15 feet from the boundary of the garden in order to prevent their roots from absorbing the nutrients the vegetable plants need.

Your garden need not all be in one location. You may grow the vegetables in one spot and the herbs in another. We grow parsley on a little spot below our kitchen's window. Any time we need some, one of us steps out of the kitchen door, cuts it, and brings it fresh to the kitchen! It is very convenient. Our guests, particularly the children, love to cut some parsley for us when we need it for the salad. To the children it is a lot of fun, to us it is a lot of satisfaction.

Good Soil

Good soil consists of 2 layers, subsoil and topsoil. The subsoil should be granular. Granular soil is essential to plant growth in several respects: (1) it allows the roots to grow with little resistance; (2) it allows water to drain fast, which prevents drowning of the roots; (3) it has the capacity to retain moisture; (4) it allows the air to circulate around the roots, which provides the roots with the oxygen they need for plant growth; and (5) it allows the carbon dioxide generated by the decomposition of the organic material in the soil to be vented into the atmosphere.

If you want to know whether a site has a drainage problem, look at it after a heavy rainfall. If water stays on the surface for a day or more, you know that drainage is poor, and that a layer of subsoil at least one foot thick needs to be added.

Subsoil should contain some minerals and organic material (explained below). If the site you choose for your garden has vegetation (weeds, lawn, etc.) on it, the soil is good enough to be subsoil. But if the site is bare or full of boulders and rocks, you should import subsoil.

Subsoil may be bought by the truckload. Some people call it "dirt" because it is not topsoil. A good source for subsoil is excavation and swimming pool contractors. You can get the address and telephone number of these contractors from the yellow pages or from friends who have bought soil before. A truckload containing 18 cubic yards may be bought for as little as $15. If the soil is of poor quality, you may get it for free, because the contractor can't find a place to dump it in. The problem with buying dirt is that it may not be available when you need it, because its availability depends on construction activity in nearby areas.

The subsoil should be overlaid by a 6-inch layer of topsoil. The topsoil should be granular and rich in organic material. The benefits of granular soil are described above. The organic material is essential because it contains the nutrients the microorganisms, earthworms, and other creatures in the soil convert into a form the plants can absorb. Soil rich in organic material is black. Organic material is described in more detail in the following section.

Topsoil is sold by the yard or by the bag. Many nurseries and garden centers sell both. The price differs greatly from place to place. In rural areas it is much cheaper. In metropolitan or rocky areas, the price can be very high. One cubic yard covers up to 50 square feet of gardening area. Buy topsoil from a reputable nursery or garden center in order to get good quality that is fertile and free of weed seeds. Do not buy it from a contractor because he may sell you screened dirt. If you have a small garden, buy topsoil by the bag. The price for a 40-pound bag varies greatly, depending on where you live and from whom you buy it. Some hardware stores sell topsoil at a competitive price.

If you find that covering the entire garden with imported topsoil is expensive, try *Theresa's Alternative Method,* in which vegetables are planted in trenches or holes that are filled with good potting soil. This method is explained later in this chapter.

If you have a small garden, buy topsoil by the bag.

Organic Material

Organic material, also called organic matter, is the product or remains of animals and plants. Cow manure, horse manure, chicken manure, tree leaves and twigs, wood chips, sawdust, grass clippings, weeds, peat moss, vegetable and fruit peels, fish emulsion, and bone meal are organic matter.

Organic material contains the nutrients the plants need to grow, but not in a form the plants can absorb. The nutrients must first be converted by the microorganisms and earthworms that inhabit the soil into forms the plants can utilize.

Organic matter benefits the plants in several respects. First, it provides food for the microorganisms (fungi and bacteria) and earthworms that convert the nutrients in the organic matter into food the plants can use. The breakdown of organic matter has 2 basic stages. In the initial stage, the microorganisms break down the organic matter into minute partially decomposed fragments. Some of these fragments contain nutrients the plants can absorb. In the second stage, the earthworms eat the partially decomposed fragments mixed with soil, digest them by their enzymes, then discharge them in the form of cast that is rich in soluble nutrients.

Second, organic matter is a soil conditioner. When integrated into the soil, organic matter loosens hard clayey soil and increases the cohesiveness and water retention capability of sandy soil. This increases the aeration, drainage, and root growth in the former and the water holding capability of the latter. And third, organic matter absorbs moisture from the air during humid days and cool nights. This nurtures the plants and saves water.

You should be aware that organic matter is perishable. It is either consumed by the microorganisms and earthworms or oxidized, meaning combined with the oxygen from the air to form carbon dioxide. Therefore, you should continually add organic material to the soil. If you don't, the microorganisms in the soil will perish and the earthworms will either die or emigrate elsewhere. As a result, the soil will harden and lose its ability to sustain plant growth.

One good source of organic matter is tree leaves. In the fall, cover the garden with as many leaves as you can, up to 4 inches. If possible, make a pass or two on them with the lawn mower before adding them to the garden. This makes their decomposition faster and prevents water clogging. Sprinkle the leaves with a mixture consisting of 2 parts lawn fertilizer and one part lime at the rate of one cup of the mix per 10 square feet. If lawn fertilizer is not available, use 10-10-10 fertilizer instead. The reason for adding lime is that tree leaves are acidic.

Tip

As a rule of thumb, add 2 pounds of organic matter for each pound of crop you harvest. Green matter such as grass clippings, weeds, and green vegetable refuse should be tilled under in order to make their nitrogen available to microorganisms and earthworms. If this green matter is left exposed, its nitrogen content will evaporate and it will turn brown. Nongreen organic matter such as tree leaves, peat moss, wood chips, and sawdust contains little nitrogen. Therefore, it should be mixed with a 10-10-10 fertilizer or cow manure before it is added to the soil. Add half a cup fertilizer or 4 pounds of cow manure for each 10 pounds of organic matter. If you don't add a fertilizer or cow manure, the microorganisms will consume nitrogen from the soil and deprive the plants of this essential nutrient.

Another source of organic matter is weeds. They are rich in nitrogen (because they are green). Cut the weeds in small pieces with a lawn mower or shovel and till them under. Do not incorporate weeds that are diseased or have seeds.

Kitchen refuse such as cucumber peel, lettuce leaves, eggplant peel, and watermelon rind is organic matter that enriches the soil. You can get a lot of spoiled vegetables from nearby supermarkets and vegetable markets. Each morning, they throw away the produce (lettuce, cabbage, spinach, etc.) that is not fit for sale. These vegetables may not be fit for human consumption, but they are excellent organic matter. Supermarkets will be glad if you take them, because this reduces the volume of their garbage.

Tip

Do not use the following organic material: (1) dog, cat, or human feces, because they may contain harmful parasites; (2) meats, fats, bones, or dead animals, because they attract animal pests, emit objectionable odor, and take a long time to decompose; and (3) grain and bread, because they attract mice and chipmunks.

Humus

Humus is organic matter that has been fully decomposed. In other words, when cow and horse manure, kitchen wastes, weeds, tree leaves, and so forth decompose completely, they become humus. Compared with raw organic matter, humus is finer and more uniform. The color of humus is very dark or black.

Humus is an excellent soil conditioner. It makes heavy soils lighter and therefore easier for the roots to penetrate and sandy soils more cohesive and water absorbent. It absorbs water from humid air, which reduces the need for watering. This is important in areas where water is scarce or expensive. Additionally, humus contains soluble nutrients and minerals.

The main source for humus is composting. If composting is not for you, buy humus from nurseries and garden centers. They sell humus in 40-pound bags at a price comparable to that of topsoil. Nurseries and garden centers sell humus alone or mixed with manure in 40-pound bags.

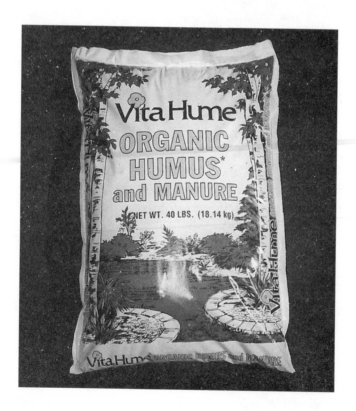

Some nurseries and garden centers sell bags containing humus mixed with manure.

Peat Moss

Peat moss is decomposed vegetation. It is an essential addition to topsoil if you grow vegetables in containers. It has little nutritive value but is an excellent soil conditioner. Peat moss absorbs 16 times its weight in water, but it dries quickly. Therefore, it should be incorporated into the soil. If it is sprinkled on the surface, it absorbs water from the soil and loses it through evaporation.

There are two types of peat moss, Canadian sphagnum and domestic sedge. Peat moss is sold in nurseries and garden centers in compressed 1- to 6- cubic-foot bales. Their price varies according to the size of the bale; the bigger the bale, the smaller the unit price. Peat moss is acidic. If your garden is acidic, add a cup of lime to each cubic foot of peat moss.

Peat moss is sold in nurseries and garden centers in compressed 1- to 6-cubic-foot bales.

Mulch

Mulch is an effective means of controlling weeds and saving water. Mulch may be organic or inorganic. Organic mulch includes bark, straw, tree leaves, pine needles, grass clippings, sawdust, wood chips, and peat moss. Newspapers are considered organic because they are made of wood.

Organic mulch should be applied after the garden is cleared of all weeds. To be effective, organic mulch should be at least 4 inches thick. With time, the mulch decomposes and becomes thinner. This causes weeds to pop through. Pull the weeds while they are still small and add more mulch to the exposed areas.

Organic mulch has several advantages: (1) it decomposes and adds nutrients to the soil; (2) it provides food and shade for earthworms; and (3) it keeps the soil cool, which is good for very-hardy and hardy vegetables. If the mulch consists mainly of nongreen material, such as sawdust, sprinkle a cup of 10-10-10 fertilizer or 5 pounds of composted manure to each 10 square feet of mulch. Also, add one cup of lime per 10 square feet of mulch if it contains a considerable amount of pine needles, because they are highly acidic.

On the negative side, organic mulch may harbor pests, including slugs and snails, especially if the weather remains damp for a prolonged period. If organic mulch gets in contact with plant stems, it may cause them to rot. Therefore, it should be kept 2 inches away from plant stems. Do not mulch heavily because it may restrict the flow of air and water to the roots of the plants.

In rural areas, organic mulch is sold by the yard. You may see for-sale signs for mulch along the roads. In urban areas, nurseries and garden centers sell organic mulches including tree bark and pine chips by the bag. The price per bag varies, depending on where you live.

The most widely used inorganic mulch is black plastic sheets. Because they are black, they inhibit the growth of weeds by depriving them of sunlight. They absorb heat from the sun during the day and thereby keep the plant roots warm during the night. This is good for tender and very-tender vegetables but not good for very-hardy and hardy vegetables (for definitions see chapter 3). In addition, plastic mulch has the advantage of conserving water and the disadvantage of restricting the amount of air and water that reaches plant roots. To improve aeration and water circulation, drill some small holes in the plastic to allow air and water to pass through.

Nurseries and garden centers sell organic mulches including tree bark by the bag.

For convenience and economy, we use plastic trash bags as mulch. They are inexpensive and easy to install. We cut 1 or 2 holes in their center to accommodate the stems of the plants and other tiny holes to let the air and water pass through to the plants' roots.

For convenience and economy, we use plastic trash bags as mulch. We cut 1 or 2 holes in their center to accommodate the stems of the plants.

Proper Temperature

Each vegetable has a range of temperature for optimum seed germination and for plant growth and production. Generally, the seeds of very-hardy and hardy vegetables germinate fastest at a temperature around 65° F (18.3° C) and the plants grow best at a temperature of about 60° F (15.6° C) by day and 45° F (7.2° C) by night. The seeds of tender and very-tender vegetables germinate fastest at a temperature of 80° to 90° F (26.7° to 32.2° C) and the plants grow best at a temperature of 75° to 85° F (23.9° to 29.4° C) by day and 55° to 65° F (12.8° to 18.3° C) by night.

The significance of this information is that growing vegetables from seeds indoors where the temperature is about 70° F (21.1° C) day and night will produce weak seedlings. By day, this temperature is too low for tender and very-tender vegetables. By night, this temperature is high for all vegetables. The high temperature during darkness produces seedlings having slim weak stems and small leaves.

Professional growers, from whom nurseries and garden centers buy seedlings, use heating and lighting equipment to provide the optimum germination and growth conditions for each vegetable. Therefore, if you want to grow seedlings indoors, you should use proper heating and lighting equipment. Seed catalogs offer such equipment. It is expensive, however. If you live in the South, you can sow the seeds of most vegetables directly in the ground.

Proper pH Value

The pH value indicates the acidity or alkalinity of the soil. The scale ranges from 0 for extremely acidic to 14 for extremely alkaline. A pH of 7.0 indicates that the medium is neutral, meaning neither acidic nor alkaline. Sweet water has a pH value of 7.0 because it is neutral.

Soils having pH value lower than 7.0 are acidic. Soils having pH value higher than 7.0 are alkaline. Each vegetable plant thrives if the pH of the soil is within a specific range. Most fruit-bearing vegetable plants grow best in soil having a pH value between 6.0 and 6.5. Most leafy vegetables thrive when the pH value varies between 6.5 and 7.0. If the pH of the soil is beyond the vegetable's range, the plants will grow poorly or not grow at all no matter how rich the soil is or how much fertilizer you apply.

If the soil is too acidic, meaning it has a pH value of less than 6.0, lime should be added. If the soil is too alkaline, meaning it has a pH value of more than 7.0, sulfur should be added. You may use pine needles, tree leaves, or peat moss to increase the soil's acidity and wood ashes to increase the soil's alkalinity organically. To know the pH value of the soil in your garden, take a sample to your county's cooperative extension office. Their telephone number is in the blue pages of the telephone directory under County Government.

There are several factors that increase the acidity of the soil with time: (1) the use of chemical fertilizers such as ammonium nitrate and ammonium sulfate and (2) in the eastern part of the United States, the acidity of the rain. This is caused by the smoke emitted by power and industrial plants in the Midwest that burn coal containing sulfur. The wind carries the smoke to the eastern part of the country where it falls with the rain and snow on the ground. As a result, the pH value of the soil decreases with time. It is recommended that you check the pH of the soil every 3 or 4 years. Some seed catalogs offer devices to measure the pH value of the soil, but our experience with these devices is not encouraging.

If the soil is too acidic, meaning it has a pH value of less than 6.0, lime should be added.

Water

Vegetable plants should be watered frequently. A rule of thumb is that vegetable plants need one inch of water per week. This is equal to one gallon per 10 square feet per day. Therefore, you must have a reliable source of water. If it rains, you can skip watering the garden for a day or two. For example, if 1/2 inch of rain falls, you can skip watering the garden for 2 days. If heavy rain is forecast, don't water the plants one day before the rain is expected.

Frequent watering is especially important after sowing the seeds or transplanting the seedlings. If the seeds are allowed to dry, they will germinate poorly or not germinate at all. If the seedlings are not watered frequently, they dehydrate and may die. On hot days, it is advisable to water leafy vegetables twice a day, once in the morning and once in the afternoon.

You need a hose and a rotary or oscillating sprinkler or a sprinkler system. Buy a good quality hose. Sprinklers are inexpensive, particularly if you buy them on sale. A sprinkler system ensures that your plants will be watered daily even when you go on vacation. If you plan to install a sprinkler system, tell the contractor to install a "high head" to water the garden. If you already have a sprinkler system and plan to establish a garden, have a high head installed.

If you have or plan to have a sprinkler system, have a high head installed.

Tip

If water is hard to come by or expensive in your area, consider putting a barrel at the bottom of each leader (downspout) to collect the water that falls on the house's roof and use it to water the garden.

Fertilizers

Fertilizers should be added to the soil to replenish the nutrients absorbed by the plants or lost through leaching, washing, or evaporation. In order to use fertilizers efficiently, you must know the nutrients each vegetable needs to grow and the benefits of each nutrient.

Plants need numerous elements to grow. Generally, all but 3 of these elements exist in the air and the soil in quantities sufficient to sustain plant growth. The other 3 elements, namely, nitrogen, phosphorous (or phosphoric acid), and potassium (or potash) are consumed by the plants in big quantities and, therefore, should be added to the soil in the form of fertilizers.

Fertilizer Classification: Fertilizers are classified as either chemical (also called inorganic or commercial), which are produced by a chemical process, or organic, which are derived from animals or plants. Organic fertilizers are explained in chapter 5.

Chemical Fertilizers

Chemical fertilizers are widely used by home gardeners because they have high nutrient content and are easy to apply and store. Their nutrients are released quickly, which ensures their timely absorption by the plants. Their chemical composition is known. For example, 5-10-5 fertilizer indicates that it contains 5% by weight nitrogen, 10% phosphorous, and 5% potassium. The disadvantage of chemical fertilizers is that they don't add organic matter to the soil. If only chemical fertilizers are used, the soil hardens, making it difficult for the roots to grow.

Some claim that vegetables grown with chemical fertilizers are inferior in taste or may cause health problems. We couldn't find anything in the literature that supports this claim. On the contrary, several references indicate that plants don't differentiate between nutrients absorbed from chemical or organic fertilizers. For example, an article by Wesley P. Judkins in the USDA (United States Department of Agriculture) *1977 Yearbook of Agriculture* states:

> Regardless of the original source, fertilizer in the soil must break down into its ionic form before it can be used by plants. The ions which are then absorbed are identical, whether derived from an organic or inorganic source.

Also, some organic gardening books claim that chemical fertilizers kill earthworms. Our experience indicates that this is not true. We use chemical fertilizers and have a very healthy earthworm population. The secret is to regularly add organic matter to the soil.

Chemical fertilizers are mostly sold in a dry form in boxes or bags that vary in weight from 1 to 40 pounds. Liquid fertilizers are usually sold in 8-ounce plastic containers. All have labels indicating their content of nitrogen, phosphorous, and potassium, in this order. The contribution of each of these 3 elements to vegetable plant growth and the harm their deficiency causes are explained as follows:

Nitrogen:
Nitrogen is vital to the growth of the green leaves. Since leafy vegetables are mostly green leaves, they need more nitrogen than phosphorous and potassium. Each time you harvest a lettuce or spinach, you remove nitrogen that has been absorbed from the soil. This nitrogen must be replaced by adding a nitrogen-rich fertilizer to the soil. If not, the plants will grow poorly.

Nitrogen deficiency causes plant leaves to turn yellow, starting with the bottom ones. After a while, the yellow leaves fall off. On the other hand, adding too much nitrogen to fruit-bearing plants causes them to grow many leaves and little fruit.

Phosphorous:
Phosphorous is essential for the growth of the vines and roots and for the formation of fruit and seeds. It also increases the plant's resistance to disease. Phosphorous deficiency retards plant growth.

Chemical fertilizers are sold in solid form in bags (top left) or in liquid form in plastic containers (top right) that have labels indicating their content of nitrogen, phosphorous, or potassium, in this order.

Additionally, the stems and leaves become reddish, then die. These symptoms start in the lower stems and leaves, then spread to the rest of the plant.

It is important to note that the plants' ability to absorb phosphorous from the soil depends on the soil's pH value (explained above). For best absorption, the pH value of the soil should be between 6 and 7. Phosphorous dissolves slowly in water. Therefore, it is better to work it into the soil a few weeks before planting.

Potassium: Potassium is essential to the plants' vigorous growth and disease resistance. It is particularly important for root crops such as potatoes, carrots, and beets. Potassium deficiency retards the growth of the plants. A symptom of potassium deficiency is that the leaves develop brown edges.

Buying Fertilizers

When buying a fertilizer, consider 2 important factors: (1) Its nitrogen, phosphorous, and potassium content. For example, a 15-30-15 fertilizer has 3 times the nutrients contained in a 5-10-5 fertilizer. Therefore, one-third cup of the former is equivalent to one full cup of the latter. (2) The content of the 3 elements with respect to each other.

Leafy vegetables such as lettuce and spinach need a fertilizer that has more nitrogen than phosphorous or potassium. If you cannot buy such a fertilizer, mix your own. For example, if you mix 1 pound of 10-10-10 fertilizer with 1 pound of 20-4-4 lawn fertilizer, you get 2 pounds of 15-7-7 fertilizer. (Do not use a lawn fertilizer that contains a weed killer, because it may kill the plants.) If you don't have a lawn fertilizer, use 10-10-10 fertilizer alone. It gives satisfactory results.

Fruit-bearing vegetables such as tomatoes, eggplants, and peppers need a fertilizer that has more phosphorous than nitrogen. Either 5-10-5 or 5-10-10 can be used. Therefore, you need to buy 2 kinds of fertilizers, one for leafy vegetables and one for fruit-bearing vegetables.

What Brand Should You Buy? One of the most frequent questions our friends ask us is what brand of fertilizer they should buy. Most mention one brand that is heavily advertised. Many believe that other brands are inferior and will produce a smaller crop. Our answer is that all fertilizers are of comparable quality. The heavily advertised brand is excellent, but its price is relatively high. Less-known brands are less expensive. Use different brands in order to diversify. We buy various brands and sizes, including 25- and 40-pound bags because their unit price is much cheaper.

Pesticides

Pesticides is a general term for chemicals that are used to kill or control weeds, insects, diseases, and fungi that harm vegetable plants. They include herbicides, which are used to prevent or kill weeds; insecticides, which are used to kill insects; fungicides, which are used to control or kill fungi; and bactericides, which are used to kill bacteria.

Pesticides are sold in different forms and sizes. Some in the form of concentrated liquid or powder should be diluted with water before application. Others in the form of dust, powder, or liquid are sprayed on the insects and diseased plants.

Pesticides are generally safe to use if you follow the manufacturer's instructions. For most pesticides, they advise not to eat the treated vegetables for a specific number of days after application. However, there is no such thing as absolutely safe. It depends on the concentration of the pesticides and frequency of use. If you use pesticides sporadically and only when the infestation or infection is serious, the harm may be negligible. But if you use them regularly, toxic material may accumulate in your body. One disadvantage of pesticides is that they may kill good insects, like bees that pollinate the vegetable plants.

Some pesticides are organic. Their advantage is that they break down quickly after application, which makes them safer to use than chemical pesticides.

Pesticides are sold in different forms and sizes.

Because a typical vegetable garden is relatively small, you can practically inspect each plant every day. This gives you the advantage of detecting problems at early stages of development and solving them without the need to use pesticides. For example, you can cultivate the weeds by hand while they are still small or use mulch to prevent their growth, instead of using herbicide. As soon as you see a diseased plant, pull it by the roots, bag it, and throw it away. If you see a few insects, pick them by hand (always wear gloves) or use an insecticide locally. The best defense against insects and diseases is a clean garden and well-fed vegetables.

Perlite and Vermiculite

Both perlite and vermiculite are soil conditioners. They have no nutritive value. Their function is to loosen the soil and improve drainage and aeration. This makes it easier for the seeds to germinate and for the roots to grow.

Perlite is a volcanic glass that has been expanded by high heat. Vermiculite is mica that has been expanded by high heat. Vermiculite holds water, while perlite doesn't. Both perlite and vermiculite are expensive. Either perlite or vermiculite is an important ingredient in potting soil and potting mix (which doesn't contain soil) if you grow vegetables and herbs in containers.

Both perlite and vermiculite are soil conditioners. They are important when growing vegetables and herbs in containers.

Potting Soil

Potting soil is the medium used to grow vegetables in containers.

Nurseries and garden centers sell bags labeled "Professional Potting Mix." These contain peat moss mixed with perlite or vermiculite and fertilizers. It is much more expensive than topsoil because perlite and vermiculite are expensive. Generally, the label on the bag doesn't indicate its nutrient content.

Nurseries and garden centers sell bags labeled "Professional Potting Mix."

Nurseries, garden centers, and some supermarkets sell 40-pound bags labeled potting soil at a price slightly higher than that of topsoil. This is in fact topsoil mixed with some organic matter. If the potting soil bags are as heavy as topsoil bags and if their price is a little more than topsoil, they are not what we mean by good potting soil.

Theresa's Alternative Method

Theresa's Alternative Method is a method of making gardening easier and less costly than the conventional method. In this method, vegetables and herbs are planted in holes and trenches dug in the garden and filled with potting soil. As a result, you don't need to till the entire area or have the whole garden covered with topsoil. The dimensions of the holes and trenches, the spacings between them, and the composition of the potting soil are given in the pertinent chapter for each vegetable.

We have been using this method of planting with great success for several years. It was inspired by our experience in growing vegetables and herbs in containers. We thought that if vegetables can be grown successfully in containers, they surely can be grown in container-like holes and trenches dug in the ground. The latter are superior to containers in several respects: (1) the size of the holes can be made bigger than the size of containers, (2) the roots can expand in the surrounding soil while they are restricted in containers, and (3) the plants can absorb more water from the surrounding area and thus require less frequent watering.

Planting Methods

There are several methods for planting. Choosing any of these methods depends on the vegetable, the size of your garden, and your preference. Three methods of planting, namely, single rows, wide rows, and hills are explained as follows:

Single Rows: In this method, seeds are sown in rows or lines that are spaced equal distances apart. The distances between the rows and between the seeds within the rows differ from vegetable to vegetable. These distances are given in the pertinent chapter for each vegetable.

If you want the rows to be straight, which gives a pleasant appearance to your garden, stretch a string between 2 stakes and sow the seeds along it. If you think this is too much work, use a stick to mark a line on the ground and try to make the line as straight as possible. With some practice, you will get it straight!

Wide Rows: In wide row planting, seeds are sprinkled at equal spacing in both directions over a wide area. The width of the row varies from 6 to 16 inches. The row's width is limited by your arm's reach to the area in the middle of the row while standing at the edges. We find that wide rows are convenient and productive for peas and beans. In addition to giving high yield per unit area, they cut down on weeds. Wide rows are also good for starting leaf vegetables like lettuce and spinach. When the seedlings emerge, they can be thinned and transplanted elsewhere. Double rows are a special form of wide rows.

Hills: In hill planting, 3 to 5 seeds are sown close to each other. They need not be sown on a formed hill, as the name implies. This method is used for planting zucchini and cucumbers.

Crop Rotation

Crop rotation is the practice of planting each vegetable in a different location each year. The advantages of crop rotation are: (1) The chances of transmitting diseases and insects to next year's crop are reduced. Specific diseases and insects attack specific vegetables. These diseases and insects move from the plants to the soil, where they winter. If the same vegetable is planted in the same spot the following year, the diseases and insects will emerge from the soil and attack the new plants. (2) Each vegetable absorbs trace amounts of specific minerals from the soil. If the same vegetable is planted in the same spot year after year, the minerals the vegetable needs to grow healthy plants will be depleted, resulting in a poor harvest. (3) The roots of legumes (peas and beans) have bacteria that absorb nitrogen from the air and fix it on the roots of the plants and in the soil. To take advantage of the nitrogen they fix in the soil, the legumes should be followed by a leafy vegetable, such as lettuce and spinach, which needs nitrogen-rich soil. This is one of the techniques organic growers use to grow vegetables without the use of chemical fertilizers.

It may be impractical to rotate every crop each year if your garden is small. This problem can be overcome by taking the following measures: (1) choose disease-resistant vegetable varieties, (2) keep your garden clean of debris, and (3) watch for insects and diseases. If a plant becomes infested with insects, pick them by hand; if a plant is infected by a disease, pull it from the ground and discard it.

Gardening Tools

Many gardening tools are available. The basic tools you need are a shovel, trowel, steel rake, tomato cages, and water hose or can. The shovel is used to till the soil, mix potting soil, move soil around, and cut the weeds if they grow big. Some gardeners use a fork instead of a shovel to till the soil, but we don't. The choice is yours. The trowel is used for cultivating the weeds, transplanting the seedlings, mixing soil or fertilizers, and filling containers with soil. The steel rake is used to grade the soil and to compact the soil over the seeds.

Tomato cages are essential for supporting tomato plants. We also use them to support running plants such as cucumbers and peas. Without them the plants will fall on the ground and their fruit will get into contact with the soil and rot. A hose or a can is used to water the plants in the garden and containers.

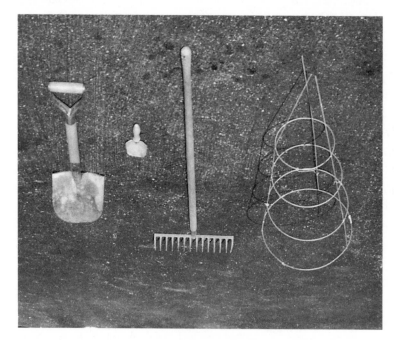

The basic gardening tools are shovel, trowel, steel rake, and tomato cages.

Proper Clothing

In the course of gardening, your footwear and clothes are likely to be soiled. You walk on dirt or mud, your clothes get in contact with plant leaves and stems, and your hands are soiled. You are also exposed to the sun. Your shoes collect mud and will soil the floor if you walk directly into the house.

Therefore, you should have a pair of old shoes set aside for gardening. Put them on before going into the garden and take them off before entering the house. Leave them in the garage or put them in a bag until you use them again. Also, have special clothes for the garden. If you don't, your ordinary clothes will be soiled no matter how careful you are. To protect your hands and fingernails from collecting dirt, use a good pair of gloves. Some are washable and can be reused.

If you like to garden during the day, you must wear a hat. The sun's ultra-violet light can cause skin cancer, particularly for fair-skinned, blue-eyed individuals. The peak of ultraviolet rays is between 10:00 A.M. and 3:00 P.M. A neighboring couple used to garden early in the afternoon, when the sun was high and hot. But they wore the proper clothing: long sleeves, long pants, and very big hats. We gave them a nickname, *the sombreros!*

Continuous Attention

Vegetable plants require continuous attention. To grow healthy, plants need to be watered daily. Weeds need to be yanked or cultivated while still small. If not, they grow fast and steal the nutrients from the vegetable plants. They also obstruct sunlight to the vegetable plants.

Fertilizers need to be added every month or when you feel that the plants' growth is slow. Their optimum use increases the yield of vegetable plants significantly.

During the harvest season, the vegetables should be picked at the peak of their ripeness. If you leave them on the vine after they have ripened, they will lose their flavor. Some vegetables including zucchini, cucumbers, and okra must be picked regularly while small. If not, several fruits grow too big and form seeds. Subsequently, the plants stop producing and die. If you go on a vacation for more than a week, have a friend look after your garden and pick the vegetables regularly during your absence.

You should watch for insects and diseases. The faster you detect them, the less the harm they can inflict. Also, watch for animal pests, especially woodchucks, rabbits, and squirrels. You may have to install a fence or a trap, if there are no laws or regulations in your area against trapping.

Chapter 3

Planning

Successful gardening starts with good planning. At the outset you should determine the size of your garden. You don't have to make a to-scale drawing or use a measuring tape. But you need to have a sense of measurement. A wide step is about 3 feet (0.915 meter). For example, a 10-step by 5-step area measures approximately 30 x15 feet (9.15 x 4.575 meters) or 450 square feet (41.86 square meters).

If you live in a rural area and have a big lot, your garden can be any size you want. The limitations will be the availability of water, the condition of the soil, how much money you are willing to spend, the amount of time and effort you and your family members can allocate to gardening, and how much fresh vegetables you and your household eat.

Next, think of the logistics and costs. If the area is heavily wooded, you will have to cut down some trees. This costs money. But you can recover most if not all the costs of cutting the trees if you use the wood in a fireplace or wood stove. If the area is bare or rocky, you have to import a considerable amount of dirt and topsoil. In addition to the price of the soil, the area you allocate for the garden should be accessible to the heavy trucks that carry the dirt and soil. Water is another factor that may limit the size of your garden. Even if everything is available, it is always better to start small the first year, then enlarge the garden's size in the following years.

If your lot is small or if you live in a townhouse (row house) where the lots are small and the land available for gardening is limited, your garden will be small. Your site will be limited to a small spot along the border of your property. Therefore, you need to choose the most productive plants, such as tomatoes, zucchini, and pole beans. And if you live in an apartment or a co-op with a balcony that receives at least 8 hours of direct sunlight per day, you can grow practically any vegetables you like in containers. Tomatoes, zucchini, cucumbers, and beans produce well when grown in big containers.

Next, you should decide which vegetables to grow and how many plants of each you need. To determine this, you need to know the minimum space each vegetable plant needs to grow and the yield per plant. These figures are given below for the most popular vegetables. The values given for plant yield are attainable if you follow the methods and recommendations given in this book and if you use good quality seeds and seedlings. Keep in mind that production is affected by factors beyond your control such as the weather conditions during the growing season.

The Space Need and the Yield of Vegetable Plants

Tomatoes: Most varieties need 10 square feet per plant. Heavy producers such as Beefsteak or Sweet 100 can easily produce 10 pounds per plant. Other varieties such as Early Girl or Celebrity are likely to produce 5 pounds per plant. The variety you choose depends to a great extent on the weather in your geographic location. If you live in a cool area like the northern United States or Canada, where the growing season is short, you may get a better crop by planting a determinate variety such as Early Girl, which matures in a shorter time and produces all the tomatoes at the same time, then dies. Regardless of where you live, always choose more than one variety unless your garden is very small.

If you live in an area where the climate is hot and the growing season is long, you are better off choosing indeterminate varieties such as Beefsteak, Beefmaster, Supersteak, Celebrity, and Sweet 100. Indeterminate varieties keep producing throughout the season until frost kills the plants. In the Tomato chapter, we expand on which varieties are determinate and which are indeterminate.

Zucchini: Zucchini is a very heavy producer. A hill consisting of 3 or 4 plants needs 16 square feet of space. Such a hill produces 20 or more pounds of zucchini, provided that you pick them regularly when small. Space and yield is practically the same for all zucchini varieties.

45

Cucumbers: Like zucchini, cucumbers are planted in hills. However, they differ in that cucumbers do best when trained on trestles or cages. This way, they need less space per hill than zucchini. A hill consisting of 3 or 4 plants requires 6 square feet and produces 4 to 8 pounds, depending on the variety. Pickling varieties produce more in number but less in weight, while slicing cucumbers including burpless varieties produce fewer in number but more in weight. Cucumbers require full sun and hot weather. If there are many cloudy days during the growing season, production drops.

Peppers: Each pepper plant needs 3 square feet of space. Production per plant depends on the geographic location, the variety you plant, and the weather during the growing season. The frying varieties do well in cool climates like the northern United States and Canada, while the bell varieties grow better in hot places like the South. Pepper plants love full sun and hot weather. If the weather is cool or if there are many cloudy days during the growing season, production suffers. When you choose the right variety for your area, and if the weather is good, each pepper plant yields about 1.5 pounds.

Onions: One onion plant needs 0.33 square foot of space. It yields either one scallion or a bulb. The weight of the bulb depends on the weather conditions. In the northern United States and Canada, the average weight of the bulb is 0.25 pound, while in the South, the average weight of the bulb is 0.5 pound. The time of planting has a significant effect on the yield. If you plant early when the weather is cool, you get a better crop.

Lettuce: A head of lettuce needs one square foot. Leaf lettuce requires on average 0.5 square foot. When the plant develops several leaves, cut every second lettuce and eat it. The rest will grow and fill the space left by the ones that are cut. Repeat this practice and you will have a good supply of fresh, tasty lettuce for several months. A full-grown leaf lettuce occupies 2 square feet.

Spinach: Spinach is similar to lettuce, but smaller. On average, each plant requires about 0.5 square foot. Early in the season, harvest every second spinach and eat it. The rest will grow and fill the space in between.

Beans: Beans are easy to grow because the seeds are fairly big. You get more yield per square foot if you grow beans in wide rows. Pole beans produce more than bush beans but they are not as tender. They also require support. Pole beans produce 0.7 pound per square foot, while bush beans produce 0.5 pound per square foot.

Peas: Pea varieties are divided into 3 groups: (1) snow peas, (2) sugar or snap peas, and (3) green peas, also called garden or English peas. (These groups are described in the Peas chapter.) All varieties grow satisfactorily from seeds if the soil is light and fertile and if you sow the seeds very early in the season, because peas grow well in cool weather. Pea production is about 0.25 pound per square foot.

Carrots: Carrots vary in length and shape to suit the type of soil. If your soil is light, plant long varieties like Tendersweet. If your soil is medium, choose a shorter and thicker variety like Nantes or Danvers Half Long. And if your soil is heavy, plant a short variety like Little Finger. Carrots produce about 0.6 pound per square foot.

Corn: For best pollination, corn should be planted in at least 4 rows spaced 2 feet apart. It is also recommended that you choose only one variety for each location in order to prevent cross-pollination. Growing corn should be considered if you have a big garden. On average, each 15 square feet produce 10 ears.

Radishes: There are 2 types of radishes, early spring and winter. The former is planted in early spring and matures in as little as 3 weeks. The latter has more varieties and takes longer to mature. The white long Japanese Daikon variety matures in 7 to 8 weeks. The radishes may be planted in single or wide rows. Because radishes sprout quickly, their seeds may be mixed with slow-sprouting vegetable seeds like carrots in order to mark the rows. One square foot produces one bunch.

Cabbage: A full-grown cabbage requires 4 square feet of space and weighs about 3 pounds. Cabbage grows well from seeds. When its size reaches 4 inches (10 centimeters) across, cut every second plant and eat it. The rest will grow and fill the space in between.

Eggplants: Each eggplant needs 4 square feet of space and yields 3 pounds. Eggplants love hot weather and full sun. Too much shade or too many cloudy days affect production significantly. It is recommended that you plant a variety that you cannot buy in the market, like the white variety or the small Italian variety that is good for stuffing.

Potatoes: Potatoes are grown from *eyes,* also called *sets* or *potato seeds.* These are pieces of potatoes containing one or more buds. Each potato plant needs 6 square feet of space and produces 3 pounds. Potatoes love light, fertile soil that is rich in potassium. You should consider potatoes if your garden is big. If your garden is small, you may plant 1 or 2 eyes for fun. If you intend to plant only a few plants, cut a few eyes from a *sprouting* potato you buy from the market. If you want to plant many, buy eyes from a seed catalog.

Okra: Okra loves hot weather. It grows well in the South and Southwest. It grows in the North if the summer is exceptionally hot. Okra is planted in rows spaced 3 feet apart. Three square feet produce one pound of okra.

Vegetable Hardiness

Vegetable plants are divided according to their tolerance of cool weather into very-hardy, hardy, tender, and very-tender. They should be planted in this sequence, i.e., starting with the very-hardy and ending with the very-tender. Please note that the hardier the vegetable, the less heat it can take. (Some gardeners refer to very-hardy and hardy vegetables as cool-season vegetables and to tender and very-tender vegetables as warm-season vegetables.)

Herbs are classified as perennials or annuals. Perennials are extremely hardy because they can take the lowest winter temperatures and be buried under the snow for months, then come back the following season. Annual herbs are classified as hardy or tender.

Very-Hardy Vegetables: Very-hardy vegetables take overnight temperatures as low as 21º F (-6.1º C). They can be planted outdoors 4 to 6 weeks before the last spring frost. Very-hardy vegetables include onions, lettuce, spinach, peas, cabbage, potatoes, and broccoli.

Hardy Vegetables: Hardy vegetables take overnight temperatures as low as 27º F (-2.8º C). They can be planted outdoors 3 to 4 weeks before the last frost. These include beets, carrots, and radishes.

Tender Vegetables: Tender vegetables cannot take temperatures below 40º F (4.4º C). Therefore, they must be planted after the danger of frost is gone. If the temperature falls below 40º F, the plants should be either covered or brought indoors. Tender vegetables include tomatoes, summer squashes, sweet corn, and beans.

Very-Tender Vegetables: Very-tender vegetables cannot take temperatures below 50º F (10º C). They should be planted outdoors 3 weeks after the last frost. Very-tender vegetables include peppers, cucumbers, eggplants, and okra.

Herbs: Perennial herbs include mint and catnip. The catnip blooms very early in the season; mint blooms a few weeks later. Annual hardy herbs include parsley and annual tender herbs include basil.

Planting Several Crops in One Season

When you know the hardiness or tenderness of each vegetable, it is possible to plant 2 crops in a cool climate and 2 or 3 crops in a warm climate each season.

In a cool climate, plant some lettuce, spinach, and onions in the area you allocate for tomatoes, peppers, cucumbers, and eggplants. By the time the latter are planted, the former will have grown big enough to be harvested,

In warm weather areas, the temperature rarely goes below freezing during winter. Therefore, it is safe to grow lettuce, spinach, and onions throughout the winter. As the weather becomes warmer, start harvesting these vegetables and plant tomatoes, peppers, cucumbers, and eggplants in their place as explained above. If you plant tender vegetables that have a life cycle of about 4 months (such as Early Girl tomatoes), you can plant a third crop in their place.

Planting successive crops in one year exhausts the soil's nutrients. These nutrients must be replenished by adding generous amounts of fertilizers and organic matter. If you fail to do so, the following year's crop will be poor. Remember, you don't get something for nothing.

Plant Arrangement

Vegetable plants vary in height from the tall corn to the short lettuce and spinach. Therefore, it is important to arrange the plants with respect to sun orientation so that the tall plants do not overshadow the short ones. This is accomplished by planting the shorter plants in the southern part of the garden, the taller plants in the northern part of the garden, and the mid-height plants like tomatoes in between. (Arrange the plants in the opposite order if you live in the Southern Hemisphere.)

To improve pollination, plant each kind of fruit-bearing vegetable close to each other. If you have hot and sweet peppers or different kinds of summer squashes close to one another, they will cross-pollinate. One year, we had green and yellow summer squashes planted next to each other. We got some fruits that were half green and half yellow.

Chapter 4

Seeds vs. Seedlings

Y ou may grow vegetables from seeds sown directly in the garden, from seedlings you grow indoors, or from seedlings you buy. Your choice depends on the climate in your area, the kind of vegetable you plant, the vegetable variety, how big your garden is, and whether you have the time, patience, and equipment to grow seedlings indoors.

Cool Areas

Cool areas freeze in winter. The northern United States and Canada are examples of cool areas. The hardiness or tenderness of a vegetable is an important factor in deciding whether to grow it from seeds sown directly in the garden or from seedlings.

Very-Hardy and Hardy Vegetables: Growing very-hardy and hardy vegetables from seeds sown directly in the garden saves time and effort. The vegetables will be ready for harvest 2 or 3 weeks later than if you grow them from seedlings grown indoors, but you will save yourself the effort of caring for the seedlings and the cost of buying heating and lighting equipment.

Growing vegetables from seedlings you buy enables you to harvest the vegetables earlier but costs money. Buying seedlings is the way to go if you plan to grow only a few plants of a particular vegetable or if you grow vegetables in containers.

Growing vegetables from both seeds sown directly in the garden and seedlings you grow indoors or buy is a middle approach. By the time you harvest the vegetables started from seedlings, those that started from seeds will have grown big enough to be harvested.

Tender and Very-Tender Vegetables: Whether to grow tender and very-tender vegetables from seeds or seedlings depends mainly on the species. To obtain the biggest harvest for the least amount of space and work, we recommend that you grow tomatoes, eggplants, and peppers from bought seedlings. Of course, you can grow them from seeds or seedlings grown indoors, but they will not be as strong and productive as those grown from good bought seedlings.

On the other hand, we recommend that beans, summer squashes, cucumbers, and okra be started from seeds sown directly in the garden. This way you save money without sacrificing quantity and quality.

Moderate and Warm Areas

Moderate areas may freeze lightly during winter. The northwestern United States is an example of a moderate area. Warm areas do not freeze in winter. The southern and southwestern United States are examples of warm areas.

Growing vegetables in moderate and warm areas is much easier than in cool areas. You can sow the seeds of practically any vegetable directly in the garden. You may start tender and very-tender vegetables from seedlings grown indoors if you want to get an early harvest or if the ground is occupied by winter vegetables. Growing from good-quality bought seedlings of vegetables like tomatoes and eggplants is recommended, especially if your garden is small.

Buying Seeds

Vegetable seeds are sold in supermarkets, hardware stores, nurseries, chain stores, seed catalogs, and discount stores. Some supermarkets, garden centers, nurseries, and hardware stores offer a discount in the neighborhood of 10%.

Seed catalogs offer the greatest variety. Their prices are not discounted but they guarantee their seeds. If the seeds don't germinate as promised, they will replace them free of charge. Our experience with seed catalogs is that they honor their guarantee. Some seed catalogs offer trial-size packets for selected vegetables at a fraction of the price of the standard packets. This kind of offer enables them to compete with discount stores and gives you an incentive to try different varieties.

Once you make a purchase from a company, they will send you 2 catalogs each year, one for spring and the other for fall. They will also sell your name to other seed companies. In no time, you will get catalogs from companies you never contacted. The names, addresses, telephone and fax numbers of some seed companies are:

Gurney's Seed & Nursery Co. 110 Capital Street, Yankton, South Dakota 57079. Order numbers: Tel: (605) 665-1930, Fax: (605) 665-9718, website: www.gurneys.com

Henry Field's Seed & Nursery Co. 415 North Burnett, Shenandoah, Iowa 51602. Order numbers: Tel: (605) 665-9391, Fax: (605) 665-2601, website: www.henryfields.com

(Note: We noticed that the products and prices of Gurney's and Henry Field's are very similar.)

Park Seed Co. 1 Parkton Ave, Greenwood, South Carolina 29647. Order numbers: Toll Free Tel: 1-(800) 845-3369, Fax: (864) 941-4206, website: www.parkseed.com

Stokes Seeds Inc. Box 548, Buffalo, New York 14240-0548. Order numbers: Toll Free Tel: 1-(800) 396-9238, Toll Free Fax: 1-(888) 834-3334.

Jung Quality Seed Co. 335 S. High St., Randolph, Wisconsin 53957. Order numbers: Toll Free Tel (credit card orders only): 1-(800) 247-5864, Toll Free Fax: 1-(800) 692-5864, website: www.jungseed.com

It is a good idea to buy seeds from a company located in a climate similar to yours.

Several chain and discount stores sell vegetable seeds for as little as 10 cents per packet. These seeds are produced by reputable companies (the name of the company is on the packet) but for some reason, they sell the seeds at a deep discount. Maybe the growers have a bumper crop or the percentage of germination does not meet the company's minimum standards. Also, there are fewer seeds in a deeply discounted packet than in the packets that sell at the regular price. Our experience with the quality of deeply discounted seeds is satisfactory.

Several chain and discount stores sell vegetable seeds for as little as 10 cents per packet.

When buying seeds, read the information in the catalog and on the packet carefully. Some seeds are labeled "hybrid," which means that they are a cross between 2 different varieties. The growers do this to get superior quality seeds. Also notice what diseases the seeds resist. It is important to choose varieties that resist as many diseases as possible. This significantly reduces the need to use pesticides. Some very-hardy and hardy vegetable seeds are labeled "slow to bolt," which means that the plants do not stop growing and form seeds when the weather suddenly turns hot. This characteristic is important for lettuce, spinach, and peas.

Saving Seeds

If by the end of the season you have some seeds left, don't throw them away, because they can be used in the following years. According to *Gardening—The Complete Guide to Growing America's Favorite Fruits & Vegetables,* published by the National Gardening Association and Addison-Wesley, the approximate storage times for vegetable seeds stored without any special moisture or temperature controls are as follows:

1 year — sweet corn, onions, and parsley.
2 years — beets and peppers.
3 years — asparagus, beans, celery, carrots, lettuce, peas, spinach, and tomatoes.
4 years — cabbage, cauliflower, eggplants, okra, pumpkin, radishes, and squashes.
5 years — cucumbers, endive, muskmelon (cantaloupe), and watermelon.

Buying Seedlings

The best place to buy very-hardy and hardy seedlings is a big nursery or garden center. The seedlings must be fresh and healthy. Those that stay on the shelves for more than a couple of days lose their vigor. Take into consideration that seedlings of some vegetables including lettuce, spinach, and tomatoes transplant well, while seedlings of others including peas and okra do not.

Most seedlings are sold in multi-cell packs or trays. First, check the bottom of the packs or trays. If the roots are sticking out of the drainage holes at the bottom, you know that the roots have overgrown their container. This is bad because it means that root growth has been constricted. As a result, the seedlings' growth will be retarded. Second, check that the stems are thick and strong, not leggy, and that the leaves are green. Long slim stems or yellow leaves indicate that the seedlings will grow poorly. Third, the seedlings you buy should be fairly big; otherwise they will take a long time to reach maturity.

Some nurseries sell pots containing one big vegetable plant, especially tomatoes and peppers, at a high price. These are OK to buy if you intend to grow a few on your balcony. However, you have to transplant them to bigger containers. They are fun but not economical for transplanting in the garden. Furthermore, they don't produce a good yield.

Time to Buy Seedlings

Buy very-hardy and hardy seedlings as soon as they are offered for sale. Usually, nurseries and garden centers start displaying them when the weather permits their transplant. Tender and very-tender vegetables are offered for sale before the danger of last frost is gone if the seller keeps them in a greenhouse. If you buy these seedlings before the minimum ambient temperature reaches the values recommended in chapter 3, you should harden them as explained below.

Hardening the Seedlings

Tender and very-tender seedlings grown in a controlled environment, whether indoors or in a greenhouse, need to be exposed gradually to the ambient temperature, a process known as *hardening*. Keep the seedlings indoors. Move them outdoors when the ambient temperature is above 65° F (18.3° C) for tomatoes and 70° F (21.1° C) for other tender and very-tender vegetables. Bring them indoors when the ambient temperature falls below these values. Gradually, let the seedlings stay longer outdoors at lower temperatures until the ambient temperature exceeds the minimum temperatures stated in chapter 3.

Chapter 5

Organic Gardening

O rganic gardening is a method whereby vegetables are grown without the use of chemical fertilizers and pesticides. Plant nutrients are provided by organic material (cow, horse, and chicken manure, bone meal, fish emulsion, fish meal, grass clippings, green manure, corn stalks and cobs, kitchen waste, tree leaves and twigs, sawdust, wood ash, sea weeds, and so on). Phosphorous is provided by ground rock phosphate and potassium by ground granite meal.

Harmful insects and plant diseases are managed by nonchemical means including keeping the garden clean, planting disease-resistant varieties, feeding the plants well, spraying the plants with nontoxic substances, and rotating crops.

Organic gardeners are conscientious people who care a lot about the environment in which we all live. They believe that we are the stewards of the earth and ought to hand it over to the next generation in the same condition if not better than the condition in which we received it from the preceding generation. *Rodale Press* is the leading publisher of books about organic gardening and they should be complimented for their efforts. If you are interested in pursuing organic gardening, write or call Rodale Press and ask for a list of their organic gardening books. Their address and toll free number are:

Rodale Press, Inc.
Department B
33 East Minor Street
Emmaus, PA 18098
Tel: 1-(800) 848-4735.

The main tools of organic gardening are organic fertilizers and composting.

Organic Fertilizers

Organic fertilizers include animal and poultry manure, green manure, bone meal, granite dust, phosphate rock, and wood ashes.

Manure

Manure (cow, horse, pig, rabbit, chicken, and so on) is the main organic fertilizer. It is sold in different forms: raw, dehydrated, and composted. Raw manure is messy and smelly and, therefore, does not appeal to amateur gardeners. It also attracts flies and other insects. Furthermore, raw manure often contains a considerable amount of undigested weed seeds. These seeds germinate and grow weeds fast because they are in a nitrogen-rich

Dehydrated and composted manure are sold in nurseries and garden centers in 40-pound bags.

environment. Controlling these weeds can be a difficult and time-consuming task.

Fresh raw manure should not be allowed to get in contact with seeds, because it inhibits their germination. Instead, it should be worked into the soil and watered frequently for a week before sowing the seeds. The advantage of raw manure is that it is cheap.

Dehydrated and composted manures are more convenient to use because they are less smelly. They are sold in nurseries and garden centers in 40-pound bags. The price of dehydrated manure is considerably higher than that of composted manure. The nutritive value of dehydrated and composted manure is written on the bag. Dehydrated manure should be watered several times before it is allowed to get in contact with the seeds. Composted manure can be applied safely at any time.

Green Manure

Green manure is a crop that is grown specifically for the purpose of plowing it under in order to add nutrients and organic matter to the soil. Some of the green manure crops are alfalfa, clover, red clover, annual ryegrass, buckwheat, Sudan grass, and oats. The former 3 crops are legumes. Their roots add nitrogen to the soil, but they take longer to grow.

Green manure crops may be planted in the summer before fall planting or in the late fall before spring planting. At least 3 weeks must pass between plowing a green manure crop under and planting a crop in its place. Green manure crops are not suited for areas that freeze in winter.

Bone Meal

Bone meal is crushed animal bones and, as such, it is an organic fertilizer. It contains little nitrogen and potassium but is rich in phosphorous. One popular brand is labeled 4-12-0. Bone meal is used as a starter fertilizer because its high phosphorous content promotes the growth of plant roots. Its advantage is that it does not burn the seeds. Its disadvantage is that it is expensive. We find that adding bone meal to the potting soil for containers improves the growth of vegetables and herbs.

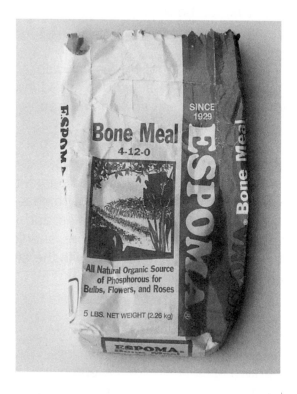

Bone meal contains little nitrogen and potassium but is rich in phosphorous.

Granite Dust

Granite dust contains 4% potassium and is devoid of nitrogen and phosphorous. Therefore, its content is 0-0-4. It takes years for granite dust to release its nutrient to the plants.

Phosphate Rock

As its name implies, phosphate rock is very rich in phosphorous but devoid of nitrogen and potassium. Typically, its nutrient content is 0-30-0. It takes years for phosphate rock to release its nutrients to the plants.

Wood Ashes

Wood ashes are an excellent source of potassium. They also have a considerable amount of minerals, especially phosphorous. Wood ashes are devoid of nitrogen because burning the wood evaporates all the nitrogen they contain. Their nutrient content varies according to the wood. Wood ashes are alkaline and therefore can be added to reduce the soil's acidity.

Shortcomings of Organic Fertilizers

Organic fertilizers have several shortcomings: (1) their price is higher and their nutritive content lower than chemical fertilizers, (2) they don't contain nitrogen, phosphorous, and potassium in the proportions that most plants need, (3) they release their nutrients slowly, and (4) there is not enough manure and other organic fertilizers to replace chemical fertilizers.

As a result of all these shortcomings, organically grown vegetables are more expensive than those grown by inorganic methods.

Composting

Composting is the process whereby organic material is converted into soil conditioner and fertilizer. It is also a means of recycling organic waste instead of sending it to garbage dumps. Composting has been used by farmers throughout the world for thousands of years. It was not until the 19th century that composting was studied scientifically.

The success of composting depends on the organic material put into the pile, the ambient temperature, the pH value of the material, the presence of moisture and air, and the size of the pile.

Organic Material

The organic material put into the pile must contain carbon and nitrogen. Carbon provides the microorganisms, mostly bacteria, that decompose the organic material with energy while nitrogen provides them with the protein they need to build their body and to reproduce.

Carbon and nitrogen must be present at a certain ratio with respect to each other. When carbon exceeds this ratio, the composting process slows down and the organic material does not decompose fully. When the partially decomposed material is added to the soil, it absorbs nitrogen from the soil to complete the composting process. This reduces the nitrogen available to the plants. When nitrogen is too high with respect to carbon, a part of the nitrogen is not utilized in the process. This excess nitrogen escapes to the atmosphere in the form of ammonia, which emits a bad odor. In addition to carbon and nitrogen, the microorganisms need moisture and minerals including phosphorous, potassium, and calcium in order to survive.

Ambient Temperature

Ambient temperature has a great influence on the composting process. During winter, when the ambient temperature is low, the microorganisms become inactive and the composting process slows down considerably. As the weather warms up, the microorganisms become more active and the composting process increases. As the microorganisms feed on the raw organic materials, they convert a part of the materials' carbon content into heat.

The temperature at the core of the pile can reach 150º F (65.6º C) or higher. This temperature is high enough to kill most weed seeds and diseases. However, the outer parts of the pile do not heat up much. This is because they are exposed to the ambient temperature, which cools them down. As a result, the material at the outside does not decompose as fast as the material in the core. The solution is to turn the pile over in order to bring the inner parts out and the outer parts in. As the composting process progresses, the temperature of the pile cools off.

pH Value

The microorganisms that decompose the organic material are most active when the pH value of the organic material is between 6.0 and 7.0. If the organic material contains too much acidic material like pine needles and maple and oak leaves, you should add lime to the pile to reduce their acidity.

Moisture and Air

Moisture and air are very important for the composting process. For the microorganisms to survive, the pile should be moist but not soggy. If rainwater is not enough, water the pile regularly. Microorganisms also need air to provide them with the oxygen they use to perform aerobic composting. Therefore, the pile should be provided with an aeration system.

Composting Methods

There are several methods of composting. Some of the widely known methods are pile composting, mound composting, sheet composting, hole composting, and earthworm composting. Pile and hole composting are discussed below.

Pile Composting

Pile composting takes place in bins. The bins may be constructed of concrete blocks, wood logs, wood blanks, or wire mesh. The walls of the bins should have spaces or holes in them to allow air to circulate throughout the pile. For best results, the compost pile should be at least 3 feet wide, 3 feet high, and 3 or more feet long. For aesthetics and convenience, the pile should be installed in an inconspicuous location very close to the garden.

You can use 1 bin, but 2 bins are preferred. Start with laying 4 to 6 inches of organic material at the bottom of the bin. Big pieces such as wood logs or corn stalks should be chipped or cut into small pieces, the smaller the better. Next, add 1 to 2 inches of dehydrated manure followed by 2 inches of topsoil. If you are using a considerable amount of acidic material such as tree leaves, sprinkle a fine layer of lime over the topsoil. Repeat this process for as long as you have organic material or until the bin is filled. The top surface of the pile should be sloped toward the center in order to collect rain water. During dry periods, water regularly in order to keep the pile moist at all times.

After about 3 months, turn over the pile in order to bring the inside material out and the outside material in. If you are using 2 bins, fill one and keep the other empty. After 3 months, move the contents of the full bin into the empty one, making sure to turn the outside material in and the inside material out. Fill the first bin with fresh organic material.

Composting will be completed in about 6 months. The process is done faster if the ambient temperature is higher and if the pile is turned over more frequently. Finished compost is then sprinkled all over the garden or used as side dressing around the plants. Compost is safe to use because it doesn't burn the plants.

Hole Composting

If you think that pile composting is a lot of work, you are not alone. As an alternative, try hole composting. Dig a hole about 1 foot across and 1 foot deep among the plants, then fill it with kitchen waste and other organic material. Add 1/2 a shovel dehydrated manure and a pinch of lime, then mix. Cover the organic material with 4 inches of soil. Each time, choose a different spot to bury the waste. Within 2 months, the organic material will have decomposed. Dig up the compost and sprinkle it around the plants.

Fighting Insects Organically

Organic gardeners rely on physical, natural, and biological means to fight insects. While tilling the soil at the beginning of the season, pick and kill any insects you uncover. Some of the insects you are likely to find are grubs, cutworms, wireworms, and slugs.

Watering the plants regularly and adequately is a natural way of fighting insects. Thirsty plants are easy prey for insects. Mulching with black plastic sheets is another means of controlling insects, because they act as a barrier that prevents insects from reaching and living in the soil.

Crop rotation is another effective means of controlling insects. Specific insects attack particular vegetables. They are often named for the vegetables they feed on the most. Some examples: Colorado potato beetles, cabbage maggots, Mexican bean beetles, and corn root worms. These insects lay their eggs in the ground in the vicinity of the plants they feed on. The following year, the eggs hatch and produce insects that attack similar crops that are planted in the same spot.

Organic gardeners also use beneficial insects to eat harmful ones. One of

An effective means of capturing Japanese beetles is the Bag-A-Bug trap.

these good insects is the ladybug. They eat aphids and scale mites. They can be bought from seed catalogs. One problem of bought ladybugs is that they are likely to fly away. Another means of killing insects biologically is to use biological insecticides. These are specific microbes that kill specific insects. More about this and other organic gardening subjects can be found in Rodale's *All-New Encyclopedia of Organic Gardening.* Rodale's address and toll free number are given at the beginning of this chapter.

Growing garlic around the plants repels many insects. Spraying the vegetables with water mixed with soap or detergent kill aphids. Laying a container of beer in the ground traps many insects.

Grubs are the larvae of several kinds of beetles, the most destructive of which are the Japanese beetles. They are ferocious eaters and can devour green leaves in no time. They keep eating even while mating! An effective means of capturing Japanese beetles is the Bag-A-Bug trap. It emits a scent that attracts the beetles, where they fall into the trap. They cannot find their way out and die. When the trap is full, replace it with another one. Close the full trap and discard it. In the first year we used this trap, it caught literally hundreds of Japanese beetles. The following year, the number of grubs in the soil and consequently the number of Japanese beetles was reduced significantly.

Managing Diseases Organically

Plant diseases are caused by bacteria, viruses, and fungi. Some of the methods used to manage diseases organically are (1) planting disease-resistant varieties, (2) keeping the plants well fed, (3) rotating the crops, (4) keeping the garden clean, and (5) spraying the diseased plants with organic substances.

Disease-Resistant Varieties

Some vegetable seeds, especially tomatoes, are bred to resist disease. The diseases the seeds resist are indicated in seed catalogs and on the packets. Read them before buying. Keep in mind that disease-resistant vegetables are not entirely immune to disease.

Feeding and Watering the Plants

Feeding and watering the plants properly is the best defense against diseases. If plants don't get enough nutrition and water they become weak and susceptible to disease.

Crop Rotation

Crop rotation is important for fighting diseases. Specific diseases attack specific plants. The bacteria, viruses, and fungi that cause the diseases winter in the soil, then attack the following year's crop. If you plant a different crop in the same spot, the chances of attack by wintering diseases is reduced.

Keeping the Garden Clean

Keeping the garden clean reduces the chances of disease infection.

Weeds can harbor some diseases that they transmit to the vegetable and herb plants in their vicinity. Cultivating the weeds at early stages eliminates this source of disease. Another measure is to pull and discard any plants that are infected. At the end of the season, remove all the debris. Do not touch the plants when they are wet because this facilitates disease transmission.

Using Nontoxic Substances

Nontoxic substances include seaweed extract, horsetail tea, garlic, baking soda, sulfur, copper, and lime. The latter 3 elements should be used with caution.

One word of caution about fighting plant diseases with organic means: sometimes they don't work. We had first-hand experience about this when a few years ago our cucumber plants were infected with downy mildew. The leaves developed big brown spots that caused the leaves to die. We couldn't find any organic cure in the literature. We tried to improvise a remedy that doesn't involve the use of pesticides. We cut and discarded all the infected leaves. That left the plants with few leaves. To encourage the plants to grow new leaves quickly, we applied heavy doses of nitrogen-rich fertilizers. New leaves grew fast but soon were infected. Next, the cucumbers were infected. Reluctantly, we had to pull and discard all the plants that year. To our disappointment, the disease appeared in the following year. We had to resort to a chemical pesticide to control the disease for 3 consecutive years. Had we known what we know now, we would have applied a chemical fungicide as soon as the mildew appeared.

Chapter 6

Earthworms: Gardener's Best Friends

Earthworms are valued as topsoil manufacturers. According to the *USDA 1977 Yearbook of Agriculture*, the earthworms in a single acre may pass more than 10 tons of dry earth through their bodies annually. This equals 0.46 pound per square foot per year. (One acre = 43,560 square feet.)

For many years, earthworms have fascinated many scientists, the most notable of whom was the British naturalist Charles Darwin. According to a Rodale book entitled *The Earthworm Book,* Darwin studied earthworms for 40 years! (Not full time, though.) He recorded their diet, feeding and burrowing habits, number per acre, and the weight of their casts per acre per year. He even conducted experiments to test their intelligence!

The number of earthworms in the soil depends on the soil's fertility and continuous supply of organic material. There may be as few as 1 and as many as 12 earthworms per square foot. On average, an earthworm produces its own weight of cast each day.

Benefits of Earthworms

Earthworms benefit the plants in several respects: (1) they convert organic material into nutrients the plants can absorb, (2) they loosen the soil, which makes it easier for the roots to grow and the air and water to circulate in the soil, (3) they increase the soil's water retention capability, and (4) they bring the mineral and other nutrients that are located deep in the soil to the top layer, where they can be absorbed by the plants.

In addition to their value to plants, earthworms are a major source of food for songbirds in early spring before the seeds and berries are ripened. Earthworms can stay alive for up to 2 weeks if kept in a dark container filled with moist peat moss.

Earthworm Species

There are more than a thousand species of earthworms. Depending on the species and the geographic location, earthworms are called night crawlers, field worms, red wigglers, red worms, English worms, red hybrid, angleworms, and rainworms. Any garden is likely to contain more than one species.

Earthworms differ in color and size. They may be reddish, maroon, dark gray, or black. Most earthworms are 2 to 10 inches long, but some species in Australia can reach 12 feet in length! You can see a photograph of these monsters in a book entitled *Earthworms, Underground Farmers*, by Patricia Lauber, published by Garrard Publishing Company in Champion, Illinois.

Feeding Habits

Earthworms thrive in moist soil that is rich in organic material. They eat partially decomposed animals and insects. Lettuce is one of their favorite vegetables. All earthworms thrive on manure.

Earthworm feeding habits differ, depending on the species. The night crawlers do not feed on the surface. Rather, they come to the surface after dusk to collect food, which consists of small pieces of organic matter or grass blades. Using their mouth, they drag what they collect into their burrow where they eat it mixed with soil. Other species including the red wigglers feed on the surface. Earthworms don't eat highly acidic or highly alkaline food.

To provide earthworms with food, organic material should be added continuously to the soil. If the organic material is depleted, the earthworms either leave the garden or die. When they die, their bodies' protein decomposes into nitrogen that is added to the soil. This benefits the plants for a short period of time but doesn't compensate the soil for the loss caused by the earthworms' death.

A few years ago, we discovered by chance that earthworms love watermelon rind. One of our favorite meals on hot days consists of watermelon, feta cheese, and a few slices of French, Italian, or pita bread. Consistent with our practice of increasing the organic matter in our garden and reducing the volume of our garbage, we cut the rind into small pieces and buried them in a spot in the garden (hole composting). Three weeks later, out of curiosity, we dug up the spot in which we buried the rind. To our surprise, we found the soil full of big earthworms. The rind was completely composted and the soil had become granular and moist. We used the soil as side dressing for the surrounding plants. Ever since, it has been our practice to bury watermelon rind in the garden, each time in a different spot.

The food the earthworms eat goes to their gizzard, where it is ground. The ground food moves to the intestine, where it is digested by the worms' enzymes. The worms use some of the nutrients in the food to grow and to fuel their activity; the rest is discharged in the form of granular cast that is rich in soluble nutrients. According to the *Earthworm Book* by Jerry Minnich, published by Rodale Press, earthworms' casting contains 5 times more soluble nitrogen, 7 times more phosphorous, 3 times more magnesium, and 1.5 times more calcium than was contained in the food the worms eat.

Life Cycle

During winter, earthworms are inactive. In areas where the soil freezes, they move below the frost line. Frost kills the worms in less than 2 minutes. In spring, when the temperature is moderate and the rainfall is plentiful, they reach the peak of their activity. They mate and lay eggs. Many eggs hatch and the small worms grow and mature. A pair of mature earthworms may produce a few hundred offspring in a year.

During summer, the worm's activity diminishes. The food available is not enough for all the worms. As a result, many of them die. The worms' survival is also affected by the amount of moisture in the soil. If the soil is always moist, the earthworms' chances of survival increases; if the soil dries, many die. In the fall the earthworms' activity increases. They lay more eggs and stay active until winter arrives and the cycle is repeated.

If unmolested, some species live for up to 10 years. However, earthworms face numerous dangers including being eaten by birds and moles, lack of food, adverse weather conditions, and the use of pesticides. As a result, some earthworms live for only a few months.

Anatomy of an Earthworm

Earthworms are considered animals even though they have no skeleton, eyes, nose, ears, hands, or legs. They sense light by special sensors. When an earthworm is exposed to light, it quickly buries itself in the ground or hides below the nearest object it finds.

Earthworms have no head but have a mouth and a brain. They have 5 connected hearts (located up front behind the mouth), blood vessels, a gizzard, and intestine. The worm's body contains 2 sets of muscles, one longitudinal and one circular.

The earthworm's body consists of numerous segments or rings. Mature worms have 115 to 200 segments, depending on the species. Each segment has 4 pairs of tiny retractable bristles. The worm uses the bristles and muscles to propel itself and to burrow.

Earthworms have a bottom side and a top side. Their skin is slimy. The slime is vital to the earthworm's survival for 3 reasons: (1) It acts as a lubricant which makes it easier for the worm to burrow. (2) It allows the worm to breathe through the skin (earthworms have no lungs). Oxygen from the air dissolves in the slime, then enters the earthworm's bloodstream. If the worm's skin dries, as when the worm is exposed to the sun or when the soil becomes dry, it cannot breathe and dies shortly thereafter. (3) It holds the worms together during mating.

Earthworms are bisexual in that they have the organs of both male and female. They reach maturity when about 4 months old, but keep growing until they are about one year old. A mature earthworm is distinguished by a thick band called clitellum (the *c* is pronounced *k*) that is closer to the head than to the tail. The clitellum plays an important role in the reproduction of earthworms.

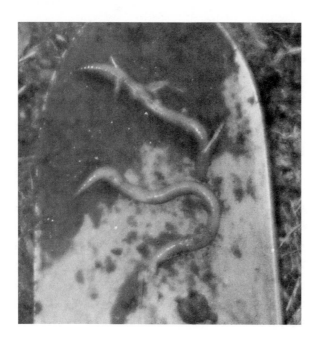

A mature earthworm is distinguished by a thick band that is closer to the head than to the tail.

Living Habitat

Most of earthworms' activity takes place in the top 12 inches of the soil, where organic debris is abundant. However, during extreme heat or cold, earthworms move downward. Some burrow as deep as 10 feet.

In soft soils, the earthworm burrows by pushing the soil aside with its body. The worm contracts its longitudinal muscles, which causes it to become thicker and shorter. Meanwhile, it anchors the bristles of its rear segments against the walls of the burrow. Next, it contracts its circular muscles, which propels the worm forward. In hard soils, the earthworm eats its way through. It swallows the soil in front of it, digests it, then discharges it from its rear end in the form of cast.

The night crawlers use the bristles to anchor their rear end to the mouth of the burrow while the rest of their body moves about the surface searching for food. If a bird or a person tries to pick them up, they contract their long muscles, which make them thicker, and cling to the burrow by the bristles. The strength of their grip and the sliminess of their body help them escape. Sometimes the pull is strong enough to break the worm. If fewer than 10 segments from the front are cut off, the worm will grow replacement rings and a mouth. If up to 25% of the worm's rear segments are cut off, new segments grow in their place. If more than these are cut off, the worm will die.

Method of Reproduction

Even though earthworms have both male and female organs, they cannot fertilize their own eggs. Two worms must mate and each fertilizes the other's eggs. When mating, both worms lie with the underside of their clitellum facing each other and their heads facing opposite directions. Mucus holds the reproductive areas together. After mating, each worm produces eggs that are fertilized by the sperms of the other. The fertile eggs are stored in sealed lemon-shaped capsules called cocoons, each containing an average of 4 eggs. The eggs hatch only when the weather is favorable. If the soil is dry or the temperature very hot or very cold, the eggs stay dormant in the cocoons and don't hatch.

Buying Earthworms

Earthworms are sold in commercial earthworm farms (not available everywhere) and through seed catalogs. Some catalogs offer a package containing 500 worms (most likely red wigglers) for a considerable price. Before considering buying earthworms, you should weigh the disadvantages. First, the worms you are likely to buy are raised in a climate and under conditions that are different from those in your garden. Second, their price is high. Five hundred earthworms sound like a lot but are not a significant quantity. You can increase the population of earthworms in your garden by many times this quantity if you add organic material to your garden.

If you start with a soil that has no worms, which is very unlikely, some will immigrate to your garden from the surrounding area. Any land that has vegetation on it is likely to contain earthworms. The topsoil you buy may contain cocoons that will hatch when the conditions are favorable. With ample organic material a pair of earthworms can multiply into 100 or more in one year. If your garden doesn't have earthworms because of lack of organic matter or because of excessive acidity or alkalinity, the ones you buy will either die or emigrate to another area.

Chapter 7

Growing Vegetables and Herbs in Containers

Most vegetables and herbs can be grown in containers. This makes it possible to enjoy gardening even if you have no lot of your own. Some townhouse (row house) and condominium regulations prohibit unit owners from gardening on the ground. The alternative is to grow plants on a balcony, deck, or patio that receives at least 8 hours of direct sunlight daily.

Although we have a garden, we grow many vegetables and herbs in containers. It seems that we got so used to growing vegetables in pots while living in an apartment that we couldn't give up the habit. Anyway, we find the practice convenient and a lot of fun. One advantage of growing vegetables in containers placed close to the house is that animal pests are not likely to come close enough to eat them.

Many of our neighbors and guests stop by to see what we are doing. They couldn't believe that vegetables can be grown in containers and produce a crop. Often, we give our amazed guests a pot or 2 of fruit-bearing vegetable or herb plants. To many of them, this would be the highlight of their visit to us. Our guests' pleasure and our satisfaction exceed the monetary value of the plants by far.

These tomatoes were grown in pots on the balcony of our apartment.

The tools for growing vegetables and herbs in containers are the right-size container for each vegetable or herb, good potting soil mix, adequate fertilizing, frequent watering, and weeding.

Containers

Containers come in different shapes, sizes, and material. The size that can be used to grow vegetables and herbs varies from 6-inch pots to huge barrels or tubs. The platform you place the containers on should be strong enough to carry their weight.

Many vegetables including peas, bush beans, lettuce, spinach, broccoli, tomatoes, peppers, and cucumbers can be grown in 10-inch pots. Most

Containers come in different shapes and sizes,

herbs including parsley, sweet basil, oregano, rosemary, and mint can be grown in 6-inch pots. We grow burpless cucumbers in 10-inch pots with satisfactory results. They produce full-size fruits, but not as many fruit per plant as those grown in the garden. We compensate for this by growing more plants. Zucchini plants are huge and therefore require big containers. We grow them in 16-inch containers with good results. Using bigger containers than those mentioned above produces a bigger crop .

You don't have to limit your choices to small vegetable varieties such as bush cucumbers and patio tomatoes. The fact is that you can grow big tomato varieties in containers. They will not grow to their full potential, but they will produce well. To prove our point, we grew a beefsteak tomato plant in a 1/2-gallon milk carton! It produced several medium-size tomatoes. Of course, the plant would have grown bigger and produced more had we planted it in a bigger container.

Most containers are made of plastic, because they are light and inexpensive. Their disadvantage is that wind can turn them over easily, particularly in the case of tall plants like tomatoes and cucumbers. Less popular are

77

clay pots. This is because they are heavier and more expensive than plastic containers. They are porous, which allows the plants to breathe better. But the pores allow moisture to evaporate, which requires more watering. Some containers are made of glazed clay. They look nice but are expensive.

Whether to buy cheap or expensive containers depends on your objectives. If you grow only a few vegetables on your balcony and want nice-looking containers, you may go for the expensive ones. But if you grow many plants as we do, then buy the cheapest containers you can find.

Look for bargains at nurseries, discount stores, and supermarkets. If you plan to grow many plants, don't spend too much money on containers. One year, a nursery was offering used 10-inch containers for 50 cents apiece. We bought a few dozen. We use them every year to grow all kinds of vegetables except tomatoes and zucchini. Another time, we found a discount store selling big plastic containers for $1 apiece. Probably they were intended for carrying laundry. We thought they could be used to grow zucchini, cucumbers, and beans and bought a dozen. The store's cashier thought that we run a laundromat! Another time, a nearby supermarket had

Snow peas produce well in containers.

Bush beans grow like magic in pots.

salad bowls in assorted colors on sale for $1 apiece. They were durable and nice looking and to us, ideal for growing seedlings indoors. We bought 6 bowls. The cashier, thinking that we would use them as salad bowls, asked if we have a very big family! We drill drainage holes in the bottom of these containers, because they were not intended to be used to grow vegetables.

Onions can easily be grown in containers.

79

You can enjoy eating fresh crisp lettuce you grow in containers.

A novelty: Growing broccoli in 1/2-gallon milk containers.

We had fun growing tomatoes in 1/2-gallon milk containers.

Peppers grow well in containers.

Zucchini produce heavily when grown in big containers.

Growing cucumbers in containers just outside our kitchen door is very convenient.

An unconventional container: A 40-pound humus bag in which we grew cucumbers!

You can enjoy eating fresh parsley grown in containers.

Growing sweet basil in containers is easy.

Potting Mix

It is important that the growing medium be very light potting mix. The reason is that plant roots will be crammed inside the container, no matter how big it is. The roots form a tight mesh that makes it difficult for the water to pass through and the air to circulate. The potting mix for each vegetable and herb is described in the pertinent chapter. Do not use topsoil from the garden, because it is likely to contain weed seeds or bacteria that inhibit seed germination. Rather, buy topsoil from a reputable nursery or garden center.

Because containers contain a small amount of soil, the nutrients, particularly the minerals, in the potting mix will be depleted by the end of the growing season. Therefore, use new mix each year.

Water

Containers are small and, accordingly, they don't retain too much water. As a result, the potting mix dries quickly. To compensate for this, the plants should be watered at least once a day. Heavy feeders such as zucchini and tomatoes should be watered twice a day, once in the morning and once in the afternoon. Lack of water even for a short period of time causes the leaves to wilt. However, they recover within an hour after they are watered. If the plants are left for a few days without water and if the weather is hot, they will die or be stunted (stop growing). Applying a mulch on the surface reduces water evaporation.

Water should be applied gently in order to prevent splashing of the potting mix. Use a can or hose that has a spray attachment. Also try not to wet the leaves of the plants during afternoon watering, to prevent diseases.

Water should be applied gently. Use a can or hose that has spray attachment.

Fertilizers

Because the containers hold little soil, the plants should be fertilized frequently. An efficient way is to use liquid fertilizer every day. Add 8 drops of a liquid fertilizer to each quart (about one liter) of water. An all-purpose fertilizer can be used for practically all vegetables with satisfactory results.

Alternatively, use dry all-purpose fertilizer at the rate of one tablespoon every 2 weeks for 10-inch containers. Increase or decrease the dose for bigger or smaller containers.

Weeding

If you use clean topsoil, it will be void of weed seeds. However, wind carries weed seeds long distances and many of them are likely to land in your containers. As a result, weeds will appear. If you don't yank them while small, they will grow fast and compete with the plants for space and precious nutrients.

Chapter 8

Pests

Two major vegetable garden pests are animals and harmful insects. The most harmful of these are explained as follows:

Animal Pests

Animal pests include woodchucks, rabbits, rats, mice, chipmunks, squirrels, deer, skunks, and raccoons. These animals' habitat and food preferences are given below.

Woodchucks

Woodchucks, also called groundhogs, are found in the northeastern United States and Canada. They are bigger than rabbits and have light brown fur. Woodchucks burrow close to food sources. Their burrow has at least 2 exits for easy escape. Woodchucks hibernate partially during winter.

Woodchucks feed twice a day, once in the morning and once in the afternoon. Their normal diet is weeds and clover, but they will gladly eat the leaves of zucchini, cucumbers, cabbage, broccoli, brussels sprouts, and collards. Woodchucks are ferocious eaters. They can eat the leaves of a full-grown zucchini plant in one sitting! Fortunately, they don't eat the leaves of tomatoes, peppers, and eggplants, but, they sometimes eat ripe tomatoes.

Our experience with woodchucks is that they eat vegetable leaves due to lack of weeds. When we moved into our house more than 18 years ago, we had an adjacent vacant lot that had plenty of weeds. A family of woodchucks had established a burrow in that vacant lot. They used to come to our garden to eat weeds. They rarely ate any vegetable plants.

A few years later, a house was built on that vacant lot. As a result, the woodchucks' habitat was destroyed. They managed to stay in the area by burrowing in a rubble fence the contractor built along the borders. With their source of food destroyed, the woodchucks started to eat our vegetables. They had no choice.

We also discovered that woodchucks have common sense. A few years ago, a woodchuck burrowed into the middle of my neighbor's vegetable garden. He used to eat from the vegetables of the surrounding gardens, but never from my neighbor's garden. It seems that the woodchuck sensed that if he ate from his landlord's vegetables, he would be evicted!

Woodchucks are shy. When they see you, they run away. But they are persistent—shortly after you leave, they come back. Dogs hate woodchucks, and a big dog can easily kill any woodchuck, regardless of its size. The only defense woodchucks have against dogs is to run and hide in the safety of their burrow.

The best way to prevent woodchucks from eating your vegetables is to construct a fence around the garden. Woodchucks are excellent diggers, so the fence should extend 3 feet below ground. Of course, a fence is an expensive solution. Another solution is to trap them if this is not against the laws and regulations in your area. Hardware stores and seed catalogs sell traps in the form of a cage. These traps don't hurt the animals. The trick is to get the woodchuck into the trap. Woodchucks take the same route every day. Put the trap in their way with some obstacles on each side of the trap, and they will enter the trap. You may use honeydew as bait because woodchucks love it. Once caught, move them to a distant place and release them, provided that local laws and regulations don't prohibit this.

One thing for sure is that we don't stand for shooting or poisoning woodchucks or any other animal pest. The punishment doesn't fit the crime. Furthermore, the poison that is intended for them may poison an unsuspecting child or adult. It is not worth it.

Rabbits

Rabbits eat the green leaves of various vegetables including beans, carrots, and lettuce. They eat the tender young bean leaves and bypass the older, tougher ones. With respect to lettuce, it seems that some rabbits have a preference. One year, the rabbits ate some of my neighbor's Butter Crunch lettuce while bypassing our Black Seeded Simpson variety. A fence will protect your vegetables from rabbits, but it may not be worth it. Trapping works; use carrots as bait.

Rats and Mice

Rats and mice belong to the same family. One difference is that rats are bigger than mice and, therefore, eat more. Both love ripe tomatoes. The solution is to pick the tomatoes as soon as they start to color. They will ripen indoors without losing much of their flavor. Also, don't include meats and grains in your compost pile.

There are many kinds of traps for mice and rats; put some in their path. Rats and mice don't like to walk or run in the open. They prefer to move inconspicuously alongside hedges and close to plants. Cats and snakes are natural enemies of rats and mice.

Chipmunks

Chipmunks eat peanuts, carrots, parsley, and other green vegetables. They like to burrow very close to food sources. They have the habit of sitting on a high rock and roaring! This makes the resident cat furious. Our late cat, Apricot, used to catch them with relative ease when they roared. However, he didn't eat them (it seems that their meat is bitter). Apricot either killed them or played with them for a while, then let them go! Chipmunks can be trapped by mouse and rat traps.

Squirrels

Squirrels don't bother vegetables much. However, they sometimes eat ripe tomatoes. The solution is to pick the tomatoes as soon as they start coloring. Cats chase squirrels, but rarely catch any. The squirrels run and climb trees faster. Squirrels can be trapped—use peanuts and peanut butter as bait.

Deer

Deer are ferocious eaters. They eat practically all vegetable plants, including tomatoes. You are likely to have deer visitors if you live near a forest or meadow. Deer are excellent jumpers; therefore, a fence should be at least 6 feet high. Deer meat is tasty. They can provide free meat for you and your family if the laws and regulations in your area allow you to kill them and provided that they are not diseased.

Skunks

Skunks are hated because of the obnoxious odor of their spray. We have heard horror stories of people and dogs who have been sprayed by a skunk. Washing the sprayed area with tomato juice helps. Generally, skunks don't spray unless attacked or threatened. Skunks are beneficial in that they eat bugs, beetles, insects, and mice. In this regard, their benefits exceed their harm. Some people use skunks as pets! Imagine what could happen if a guest or a child bothered them.

Skunks can be trapped, but we don't recommend that for fear of being sprayed. If your trap catches a skunk, cautiously release it without making any aggressive move. Once again, be very calm and very cautious. It is a good idea to cover every inch of your body before approaching a trapped skunk!

Raccoons

Raccoons do little harm to vegetable gardens. Like skunks, they love melons. They feed mostly by night. They are shy and run when a human approaches them. Some raccoons are rabid, and those that carry the disease tend to be docile and friendly. If a raccoon shows such behavior, don't come close to it. Raccoons can be trapped. Only a big dog can attack a raccoon. When attacked by a dog, the raccoon jumps on the dog's back to gain the upper hand!

Harmful Insects

Harmful insects are numerous. The damage they inflict on vegetable plants varies from negligible to severe. We will explain in the following section some of these insects, the damage they can inflict on plants, and the best method of controlling them. Ortho Company has a chart in color that illustrates most harmful insects and the insecticide that kills each. You may be able to get a free copy of this chart from a nearby big nursery.

Japanese Beetles

Japanese beetles are recognized by their metallic dark brown color. They emerge from grubs that lie in the ground during winter and spring. The grubs are light gray with a little brown head. They usually stay in a coiled-up position.

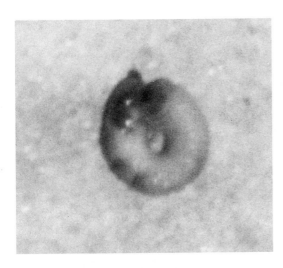

Japanese beetle grubs are light gray with a little brown head. They usually stay in a coiled-up position.

As grubs, they feed on the roots of the plants. As beetles, they devour the green leaves of many vegetables. If your garden is infested with Japanese beetles, you will uncover many grubs while tilling the soil in early spring before planting. Pick and kill any grubs you encounter. The best way to control the beetles is by the Bag-A-Bug trap described in chapter 5.

Cutworms

Cutworms look like Japanese beetle grubs, but they are bigger. Early in the season, they chew the stems of young seedlings at ground level. In summer, they climb up some plants and dig holes in the fruit. They attack several plants including tomatoes, cabbages, broccoli, and peppers. Pick them while tilling the soil at the beginning of the season. If you find that they are numerous, you may have to use an insecticide. Cutworms can be controlled by placing a collar around the stem of each seedling.

Aphids

Aphids are tiny insects that suck the sap of the plant leaves. They feed on lettuce, parsley, and other leafy vegetables. The best way to control them is to wash both sides of the leaves with a strong spray of water. If they are persistent, add some soap to the water. We don't recommend using an insecticide to control aphids unless their infestation is severe.

Mexican Bean Beetles

Mexican bean beetles are oval-shaped and about 3/8-inch long. They look like ladybugs. Their color is yellow-brown with 16 black spots on their back. Mexican bean beetles attack all bean varieties, feeding on the leaves. Handpick them if they are few. If they are many, an insecticide may have to be used.

Colorado Potato Beetles

Colorado potato beetles chew the leaves of several vegetable plants, especially potatoes and eggplants. This retards the growth of the plants. If picking them by hand is not effective, you may have to use an insecticide.

Cabbage Loopers

Cabbage loopers are 1 1/4-inch green caterpillars. They are the larvae of moths that fly by night. They move by pulling their rear end forward while arching their back, then looping their front end forward. They feed on the leaves of cabbages, cauliflower, broccoli, brussels sprouts, lettuce, spinach, and beets. Pick and destroy the caterpillars if they are few. If their numbers increase, use an insecticide.

Corn Earworm

Corn earworms are 1 1/2-inch green caterpillars with longitudinal brown and green stripes. They feed on the silk and kernel close to the silk. They also feed on beans, potatoes, squashes, and peppers. Because the damage they inflict on corn can be serious, you may have to apply an insecticide early in the season.

Chapter 9

The Contribution of Home-Grown Vegetables to Good Health

Home-grown vegetables and herbs are rich in vitamins, minerals, and fiber. These nutrients are essential to good health and a strong immune system. By contrast, the vegetables and herbs we buy are deficient in these important nutrients. The reason for the deficiency is that the vegetables and herbs sold in the market are treated with pesticides which deplete their vitamin content. Also, vegetables and herbs lose a significant portion of their vitamin content during transportation and while staying on the shelves for an extended period of time.

It is a widely known fact that most tomatoes sold in the market are picked green, then sprayed with a gas to give them red color! In addition to being tasteless, these tomatoes contain few vitamins, because they did not ripen on the vines. By contrast, the vegetables and herbs you grow maintain most of their vitamin content, because you pick them at the peak of ripeness and because you don't spray them with any pesticides unless absolutely necessary.

In this chapter, we explain the important role vitamins, minerals, and fiber play in good health, the effect of their deficiency on our health, and the vegetables and herbs that contain them.

Vitamins

Vitamins are essential to good health. Without them, we fall sick and die. They assist in converting the nutrients in the food we eat into energy. Additionally, they boost our body's immune system, which is our major defense against diseases. Several vitamins are antioxidants, meaning they neutralize the free radicals (explained below) that damage our body's cells. In this regard, they protect our body against illnesses including cancer and heart diseases. Detailed explanation of the immune system can be found in many references. Two of these references are: (1) *Prescription for Nutritional Healing* by James F. Balch, M.D. and Phyllis A. Balch, C.N.C. and (2) *The Mount Sinai School of Medicine Complete Book of Nutrition*, edited by Victor Herbert, M.D., F.A.C.P. and Genell J. Subak-Sharpe, M.S.

Getting vitamins from vegetables and herbs is better than getting them from supplements. According to reference 2 mentioned above, "the high concentration in the intestine of a vitamin or mineral in pills interferes with the absorption of some other nutrients." Additionally, fresh vegetables and herbs contain a multitude of vitamins, while pills contain only the nutrients listed on the label.

To get the optimum amount of vitamins, vegetables and herbs should be eaten raw as much as possible. Cooking and processing kills a significant portion of the vitamins contained in the food .

There are 13 vitamins. Four of them (A, D, E, and K) are fat soluble. They are stored in the liver and fat tissue of the body. The other 9 vitamins, namely vitamin C and 8 B vitamins are water soluble. They are stored in the body for only a short period of time. Any amounts unused by the body are discharged mostly in the urine.

Vitamin A and the Carotenoids

Vitamin A and the carotenoids are closely related. Some carotenoids are converted in the liver into vitamin A as needed. Fresh vegetables contain numerous carotenoids, the most widely known of which is beta carotene. It has been widely described as the most important and safest form of carotene, but recent studies indicate that all carotenoids are essential to good health. They can be obtained only from fresh vegetables.

Vitamin A is known as the "eye vitamin" because it prevents night blindness. It is also good for the skin, hair, nails, bones, teeth, gums, and glands. It helps the body resist cancer. Vitamin A increases the body's resistance to colds and infection. Both vitamin A and the carotenoids are important antioxidants. They protect the body from the free radicals that damage body cells. They strengthen the immune system and attack cancer-causing substances. Furthermore, they are credited with reducing heart diseases and strokes.

Deficiency in vitamin A causes night blindness, dry eyes, dry hair and skin, fatigue, and loss of memory. Vitamin A withstands the high temperature of cooking, although a significant portion can be destroyed at 275° F (135° C). Boiling does not destroy vitamin A but pressure cooking does. When the vegetables and herbs lose their freshness, they lose their vitamin A and carotenoid content.

The vegetables and herbs that contain the highest amount of vitamin A and carotenoids are carrots, sweet potatoes, cantaloupes, dandelion, and parsley. Eating a few fresh carrots a day provides your body with all its needed vitamin A and the carotenoids.

B Vitamins

B vitamins include 8 vitamins that work best when taken together. They are essential for a healthy nervous system, muscle tone, digestion, energy, skin, and mental and emotional functions. Some reports suggest that there is a connection between Alzheimer's disease and deficiency in B vitamins. Stress depletes B vitamins in our body. Therefore, if you work in a stressful job, eat a lot of vegetables that contain B vitamins.

The 8 vitamins that constitute B vitamins are B_1, B_2, B_3, B_5, B_6, B_{12}, biotin, and folic acid. A brief description of the benefits of these vitamins, the illnesses caused by their deficiency, and the vegetables and herbs that contain them are explained in the following:

Vitamin B_1 (Thiamine): Vitamin B_1 helps convert the starch and sugars in the food we eat into energy. It is also good for the healthy function of the brain, stomach, and nervous system, and for muscle tone. Food processing, cooking, chlorine in the drinking water, and a diet high in fat, sugar, coffee, and alcohol and low in fiber depletes the vitamin B_1 in our body.

Deficiency in vitamin B_1 causes fatigue, constipation, and weakness. Good sources of vitamin B_1 are peas, beans, corn, dandelion greens, beet greens, brussels sprouts, okra, broccoli, potatoes, carrots, and asparagus.

Vitamin B_2 (Riboflavin): Vitamin B_2 is necessary for good vision, healthy skin, nails, and hair, and red blood cell formation. It aids in digestion and in converting the calories in the food we eat into energy. Its deficiency makes the eyes sensitive to light, causes cracks and sores around the mouth, and makes it difficult to eat and swallow. The vegetables and herbs that are rich in vitamin B_2 include beet greens, broccoli, leafy greens, and watercress.

Vitamin B_3 (Niacin or Niacinamide): Vitamin B_3 is important for healthy skin and for the proper functioning of the digestive and nervous systems. It helps convert the calories in the food we eat into energy. It lowers cholesterol and improves blood circulation. Deficiency in B_3 causes fatigue, depression, mouth sores, diarrhea, headaches, and indigestion. The vegetables and herbs that are rich in vitamin B_3 include broccoli, dandelion greens, carrots, potatoes, tomatoes, parsley, and peppermint.

Vitamin B_5 (Pantothenic Acid): Vitamin B_5 is known as the anti-stress vitamin. It is important for digestion and helps convert the calories in the food we eat into energy. It also helps our body resist diseases. Its deficiency causes fatigue and headache. The vegetables that contain B_5 include peas and beans.

Vitamin B_6 (Pyridoxine): Vitamin B_6 is essential for metabolism of fats and protein and for the production of red blood cells. It is also impor-

97

tant for muscle and brain functions. Some reports suggest that B_6 helps the body fight cancer and arthritis. Deficiency in vitamin B_6 causes headaches, dizziness, fatigue, depression, scaling skin, and hair loss. The vegetables that contain vitamin B_6 include carrots, spinach, cabbage, beans, corn, broccoli, and potatoes.

Vitamin B_{12}: Vitamin B_{12} prevents anemia. It is essential for the normal function of all body cells and for the formation of red blood cells. Deficiency in B_{12} causes fatigue, loss of appetite, nervousness, sore tongue, hard breathing, pain in swallowing, and memory loss. Vegetables, with the exception of soybeans, are void of vitamin B_{12}. Therefore, pure vegetarians should take B_{12} supplements.

Biotin: Biotin is essential to metabolism of fats, carbohydrates, and proteins. It is important for healthy skin and hair and for relieving muscle pain. Vegetables and herbs are not an important source of biotin.

Folic Acid (Folate or Folacin): Folic acid is important for converting the calories in the food we eat into energy and for forming red blood cells. It is involved in the formation of white blood cells, a major component of the immune system. A recent study indicates that folic acid helps prevent breast cancer. It is also important for pregnant women in that it helps in the formation of the nervous system of the fetus, and in the prevention of premature birth. Its deficiency causes anemia, sore tongue, fatigue, and loss of memory. Folic acid is contained in broccoli, lettuce, spinach, beans, peas, and potatoes.

Vitamin C (Ascorbic Acid)

Vitamin C is a major antioxidant. It is essential for a strong immune system and healthy gums. It protects the body from the effects of pollution and other cancer-causing agents. It increases the body's ability to absorb iron. Some reports suggest that vitamin C reduces cholesterol and high blood pressure. A recent study indicates that vitamin C is important in fighting stress. Alcohol, smoking, and oral contraceptives deplete vitamin C in our body.

Deficiency in vitamin C causes bleeding gums, poor teeth, rough skin, fatigue, loss of appetite, susceptibility to infection, poor digestion, and prolonged healing time. Green peppers are very rich in vitamin C. Other vegetables and herbs that contain vitamin C include broccoli, brussels sprouts, dandelion greens, green peas, tomatoes, watercress, spinach, and peppermint.

Vitamin D

Vitamin D is essential for the absorption of calcium and phosphorous by our body. This is the reason most of the milk we buy is fortified with vitamin D. Additionally, vitamin D prevents muscle weakness and strengthens the immune system. Deficiency in vitamin D causes diarrhea and loss of appetite.

The vegetables and herbs that contain vitamin D include sweet potatoes, parsley, and dandelion greens. The sun is a good source of vitamin D. You can get all the vitamin D your body needs if you expose your face and arms to the sun for an average of 10 minutes daily.

Vitamin E

Vitamin E is a potent antioxidant. It enhances the body's ability to prevent cancer and heart diseases and reduces the harmful effects of the breakdown of unsaturated fats. It helps red blood cells live longer and speeds up wound healing. Some reports suggest that vitamin E retards the aging process and Alzheimer's disease. Deficiency in vitamin E shortens the life span of red blood cells and damages the nerves. The vegetables and herbs that contain vitamin E include spinach, watercress, sweet potatoes, lettuce, and dandelion.

Vitamin K

Vitamin K is not as widely known as other vitamins, but it is important in several respects. First, it is necessary for blood clotting. Second, it helps the development and maintenance of the bones. Third, it is good for the liver. Some reports indicate that it helps the body resist cancer. Its deficiency can cause internal bleeding and liver damage. The vegetables that contain vitamin K include broccoli, brussels sprouts, cabbage, spinach, and lettuce.

Minerals

Minerals are essential for the formation of bones, teeth, and blood and for the maintenance of healthy muscles and nerves. They regulate the heartbeat and are involved in delivering oxygen to body cells.

Earth is the source of all minerals. Plants absorb minerals from the soil. When we eat the plants, we absorb the minerals contained in them. (We also get minerals from animals that got their minerals from plants.) The most important minerals and the vegetables and herbs that contain them are explained in the following:

Calcium

Calcium is essential for strong bones and teeth and for healthy gums. It regulates heartbeat and helps maintain proper blood, muscle, and nerve functions. It helps convert the calories in the food we eat into energy and helps the blood to clot. Calcium deficiency causes loss of bones, tooth decay, brittle nails, arthritis, and aching joints. The vegetables and herbs that contain calcium include spinach, lettuce, dandelion greens, parsley, broccoli, cabbage, beet greens, mustard greens, and watercress.

Iron

Iron is essential for the production of blood hemoglobin, which carries oxygen to all body cells. It increases resistance to stress and diseases and is important for muscle and bone formation. Iron deficiency causes fatigue, shortness of breath, weak bones and muscles, and dizziness. The vegetables and herbs that contain iron include spinach, lettuce, potatoes with skin, and peppermint.

Magnesium

Magnesium is essential for converting the food we eat into energy and for maintaining healthy muscles and nervous system. It is also important for strong bones and teeth. Magnesium deficiency causes poor digestion, heart problems, weak muscles, and cramps. The vegetables and herbs that contain magnesium include lettuce, spinach, corn, garlic, watercress, parsley, mint, and catnip.

Manganese

Manganese converts the food we eat into energy, strengthens the immune system, and regulates blood sugar. It is important for the proper functioning of the reproductive organs and for healthy bones. Its deficiency causes high cholesterol, hearing problems, and eye and ear infections. The vegetables and herbs that contain manganese include lettuce, spinach, peas, beans, dandelion, parsley, mint, and catnip.

Phosphorous

Phosphorous is essential for bone and tooth development, for growth and maintenance of body cells, heart, kidney and brain functions, heart muscle contraction, and transmission of nerve impulses to the brain. Deficiency in phosphorous causes fatigue, bone pain, and irregular breathing. The vegetables and herbs that contain phosphorous include beans, peas, corn, and garlic.

Potassium

Potassium is important for body growth and proper functions of the brain, heart, and nervous system. It is essential for healthy skin. It works with sodium to maintain the balance of body fluids. Potassium deficiency causes constipation, dry skin, low blood pressure, fatigue, depression, and headaches. The vegetables that contain potassium include corn, beet greens, beets, spinach, potatoes, broccoli, cabbage, cauliflower, lettuce, peas, beans, and tomatoes.

Selenium

Selenium is a powerful antioxidant. It works with vitamin E to maintain the health of the heart and liver. Some reports claim that it resists Alzheimer's disease. Selenium deficiency reduces the body's resistance to cancer and heart disease. The vegetables and herbs that contain selenium include broccoli, onions, garlic, parsley, peppermint, and catnip.

Sulfur

Sulfur disinfects the blood and fights harmful bacteria. It is important for hair and nail formation. It protects the body against radiation and pollution. Some reports suggest that it slows down the aging process. The vegetables and herbs that contain sulfur include onions, garlic, cabbage, and brussels sprouts.

Zinc

Zinc is important for development of the reproductive organs. It strengthens the immune system and is vital for bone development. Zinc deficiency adversely affects the nails, hair, prostate, and the body's resistance to infection. The vegetables and herbs that contain zinc include peas, beans, and parsley.

Fiber

Fiber is gaining wide medical attention as a means of lowering cholesterol, stabilizing blood sugar, and removing heavy metals from the body. Because it is a laxative, fiber reduces the chances of colon cancer and prevents constipation. Constipation is the cause of many ailments including varicose veins, hemorrhoids, gas, fatigue, headache, and bad breath. The vegetables that contain fiber include lettuce, spinach, potatoes with skin, peas, and beans.

Free Radicals

Free radicals are oxygen molecules that have only one electron in their outer orbit instead of the usual 2. This makes these molecules unstable. To gain stability, a free radical grabs an electron from a neighboring oxygen molecule in one of the body cells. This damages the cell. The neighboring molecule that has lost an electron becomes a free radical. It grabs an electron from a neighboring molecule and the destructive cycle continues. Each free radical exists for only a small fraction of a second, but the damage it causes to body cells is permanent. Free radicals weaken the immune system, which leads to infection, heart disease, cancer, and aging.

Free radicals are produced naturally by the body in the process of converting the food we eat into energy. Dietary factors that cause free radicals to be produced in great numbers include eating a diet rich in fat, refined sugars, sugar substitutes, and alcohol, as well as smoking and cooking food at a high temperature, especially grilling. Free radicals are also caused by environmental factors including air pollution, ozone, radiation, pesticides, excessive exercise, and some medication.

Antioxidants

Antioxidants are a group of vitamins and minerals that neutralize the free radicals by converting them into water and ordinary oxygen. The major antioxidants are vitamin A, beta carotene, vitamin C, vitamin E, selenium, and zinc.

When we are young, our body produces sufficient amounts of antioxidants to neutralize the free radicals. As we grow older, our body's production of natural antioxidants diminishes. To offset this, we should eat more fresh raw vegetables and herbs, especially those that contain antioxidants.

Part 2

Very-Hardy Vegetables

Chapters in This Part

Chapter 10

Onions

Onions are versatile. They can be eaten green, raw, pickled, fried, broiled, and in salads and breads. Onions can also be used to season tomato sauces and stews, and to spice shish kabobs. They are excellent in seasoning chicken, turkey, and lamb because they absorb these meats' greasy odor. Cut an onion in quarters and place it in the cavity of a chicken or turkey before roasting it and you will notice a big improvement in the taste. For best-tasting grilled chicken and lamb, marinate them in onion juice for a few hours or overnight before grilling. Not surprisingly, onions rank third in popularity among home gardeners—just behind tomatoes and peppers.

Time to Plant Onions

In cool areas like the northern United States and Canada, the time to plant onions is from early to mid spring, the earlier the better. In the areas that don't freeze, like the South and Pacific West, onions can be planted in the fall for winter harvest and in early winter for spring harvest. To extend the green onions' harvest season, make successive plantings every 2 weeks.

General Information Concerning Onions

Onions require light, fertile, limed, and weed-free soil. They may be harvested as green onions, also called scallions, or bulbs. Each kind requires different ambient temperature. The green tops grow best in cool weather, while big bulbs grow best in warm weather. Therefore, if you start planting onions early you get a good crop of both. Any onion variety can be har-

Any onion variety can be harvested as green onions.

vested as green onions. However, some varieties are bred specifically for this purpose. They are called *bunching,* because they are sold in bunches.

Onions' pungency is proportional to their sulfur content. The most important factors that affect an onion's pungency are the variety and the chemical composition of the soil. For example, the famous Vidalia onions are grown best in certain areas in Georgia whose soil is favorable for growing this variety.

Onions may be grown from sets, seedlings, or seeds. Sets are small bulbs that were harvested the previous year when they were small. They are the easiest and fastest way to grow onions and the best in resisting diseases. They sprout in a matter of days and can be harvested as green onions 4 to 5 weeks after planting. However, sets do not produce big bulbs.

Onion sets are sold in nets (for aeration) each containing 75 to 100 sets. They are labeled as yellow, white, or red. The yellow is the most popular.

Onion sets are sold in nets, each containing 75 to 100 sets.

Onion sets are sold in garden centers, discount stores, nurseries, and seed catalogs. Some sell a net containing a nominal 100 sets for as little as 99 cents. Out of curiosity, we counted the number of sets in one net and found 132, less than one cent per set! You cannot beat this price.

When buying onion sets, choose ones that are firm. Soft sets or those that have sprouted do not grow well. The set should not be more than 3/8 inch in diameter. Small sets produce big bulbs, while big sets produce small bulbs. Therefore, plant small and big sets separately. Harvest the big sets as scallions and leave the small ones to form bulbs. Onion sets may be round or elongated. Round sets produce flattened bulbs, while elongated sets produce round bulbs.

Seedlings are the second easiest to grow. They form bigger bulbs than those grown from sets. Nurseries and garden centers sell seedlings at a reasonable price, but they offer a limited variety. Seed catalogs offer a great variety but their price is high. The seedlings you buy must be strong and fresh. Those that stay on the shelves for more than a couple of days or the ones that have turned yellow will not grow.

Onion seeds are the most difficult to grow. They are hard to germinate and require a long time to grow. You can buy onion seeds from nurseries, garden centers, discount stores, or seed catalogs. The latter offer the greatest variety. Onion seeds are classified as "*short-day,*" meaning they grow best in the South, or "*long-day,*" meaning they grow best in the North. The further north you are, the longer the summer days. (If you live in the Southern Hemisphere, the opposite is true.) The bulbs of short-day onions begin to form when daylight becomes 12 hours or longer. The bulbs of long-day onions start to form when daylight becomes 14 hours or longer. For your information, the longest day of the year is June 21, which is the beginning of summer.

Preparing the Soil for Onions

The Conventional Method: A week before planting, work some organic material such as peat moss, humus, or composted manure into the top 8 inches of the soil at the rate of 4 pounds per 10 square feet. Double this rate if the soil is hard, or if the plot was not used for growing vegetables before. Next, sprinkle 5-10-10 fertilizer at the rate of one cup per 10 square feet. Water thoroughly.

Theresa's Alternative Method: In the area you designate for onions, dig 8-inch-deep trenches 12 inches apart. The width of the trenches should be 5 inches for single-row planting and up to 16 inches for wide-row planting. You may dig trenches for some of the onions you intend to harvest as green onions in the area where you intend to grow tomatoes and peppers. By the time these plants grow big, the onions will have been harvested.

Prepare potting soil consisting of one part by volume clean topsoil, one part peat moss, and one part composted manure. Additionally, add one cup 5-10-10 fertilizer and 1/2 cup lime to each cubic foot of potting soil, then mix well. Fill the trenches with the mix, then water thoroughly for a few days.

If you plan to grow onions in containers, replace the composted manure with one part perlite or vermiculite and add one cup of bone meal to each cubic foot of the mix.

Planting Onions

In the conventional method, plant onions in rows 12 inches apart. In Theresa's alternative method, plant onions in the trenches you filled with potting soil. In both methods, plant the sets 2 inches apart for green onions and 4 inches apart for bulbs. If you like to eat both, plant the sets every 2 inches. When the green tops grow big enough, pull every second plant and eat it as a green onion, leaving the rest to form bulbs. Be careful not to disturb the roots of the remaining plants. Onion sets should be planted 1 to 2 inches deep, with their pointed end facing up. They should be covered completely with soil.

If you grow onions from seedlings, use the same distances as for bulbs. Transplant the seedlings immediately after buying them. Before transplanting, the seedlings should be watered generously and allowed to stand for at least an hour. It is recommended that you transplant the seedlings on a cloudy day or after sunset to reduce the chances of plant dehydration.

If you want to grow onions from seedlings grown indoors, start 6 to 8 weeks before the soil can be worked. Fill a flat or a container with good potting soil as described above in Theresa's alternative method. Water thoroughly for a couple of days. Next, sprinkle the onion seeds evenly, then cover them with 1/4 inch potting soil. It is recommended that you use 2 or more seed varieties. If one variety doesn't germinate well, the other will. Don't worry about the cost of the seeds.

To grow onions from seeds sown directly in the garden, sow the seeds 1/2 inch apart and 1/4 inch deep.

After planting either sets, seedlings, or seeds, firm the soil over them with a rake or the back of a shovel. Water thoroughly. If rain is forecast, Mother Nature will water your onions for free!

Caring for Onions

It is important that you keep the area around the onions free of weeds. Using clean potting soil as suggested in Theresa's alternative method delays the emergence of weeds, but not for long. Wind carries weed seeds everywhere. When the weather warms up, the weeds appear. It is easier to cultivate the weeds when they are tiny and when the soil is wet. They can be yanked without disturbing the roots of the onions. Just be careful.

If the seedlings grown from seeds sown directly in the ground are close to each other, thin them to the distances explained earlier.

Water the onions every day in order to get a good crop. Fertilize them every month with a 5-10-10 fertilizer at the rate of one cup per 10 feet of single row. Watch for diseases and insects. Pull the infected or infested plants with their roots, then bag and discard them. We don't recommend using a chemical pesticide to fight onion insects. It is cheaper, and definitely safer, to pull and discard the infected plants.

Harvesting Onions

Green onions can be harvested when they reach 10 to 12 inches high. This may take as little as 4 weeks from the time of planting the sets. Hold the plants at ground level and pull them out gently. They come out easier if the soil is moist. If you have started early from sets, you can plant other sets in place of the ones you harvest.

Bulbs reach their maximum size when the leaves start to turn brown. To speed maturity, bend the leaves horizontally at the ground level by hand or with the back of a rake. Leave the bulbs in the ground for a few more days, then pull or dig them up. Let them dry up in a dry, warm, and airy location for a couple of weeks. Onions should be stored in a cool and dry spot.

Onion Diseases

Onion diseases include downy mildew, nematodes, dry rot, root rot, and bacterial rot.

Onion Insects

The insects that attack onions include onion maggots and thrips. The former is a problem in the North. They thrive when the weather remains humid for a long period of time. The latter thrive during hot dry weather.

Onion Varieties

Long-day: Long-day varieties include Yellow Sweet Spanish, White Sweet Spanish, Dulce Grande, Columbia, First Edition, and Walla Walla Sweet.

Short-day: Short-day varieties include White Bermuda, Giant Red Hamburger, Vidalia, Yellow Granex, Candy, Red Grano, and Texas Grano.

Bunching: Bunching varieties include He-Shi-Ko, White Bunching Onions, Tokyo Long, White Lisbon, Feast, and Southport White.

Nutritive Value of Onions

Onion bulbs contain vitamin C, potassium, phosphorous, and calcium. Green onions are rich in vitamins A and C and in potassium, phosphorous, calcium, and fiber. Both green onions and bulbs contain sulfur, which protects the body from pollution and radiation. Both contain 10 calories per ounce.

Chapter 11

Lettuce

There is no comparison between the taste, freshness, and nutritive value of the home-grown lettuce and the ones you buy at super-markets and vegetable stores. You can grow one or more of the tender varieties that are available. Fortunately, lettuce is easy to grow from seeds sown directly in the garden. The secret lies in the soil and planting time.

Time to Plant Lettuce

In cool areas like the northern United States and Canada, the time to sow lettuce seeds in the garden is early spring as soon as the soil can be worked. In areas that don't freeze, like the South and Pacific West, lettuce may be sown in the fall for winter harvest and in winter for spring harvest. To extend the harvest season, make successive plantings every 2 weeks but stop when the weather becomes warm, because the seeds will not germinate.

General Information Concerning Lettuce

Lettuce needs soil that is rich in humus and nitrogen. There are many lettuce varieties. They are divided into 4 groups: *looseleaf, cos or romaine, crisphead or iceberg, and butterhead or Boston.* The names of some varieties in each group are given later in this chapter. The nutritive value of lettuce depends on the variety. The iceberg contains the smallest amount of nutrients.

Lettuce may be grown from seeds sown directly in the garden, from seedlings grown indoors, or from seedlings you buy.

Lettuce seeds may be bought from seed catalogs, nurseries, garden centers, supermarkets, or discount stores. Each packet contains between 500 and 1,000 seeds. Some seed catalogs and supermarkets sell seeds at a discount, particularly at the end of the season. Since lettuce seeds can be used the following years, it is a good idea to buy some packets for the following year.

To save money, you can buy lettuce seeds at a deep discount from several national and local discount stores. Some stores sell seeds for as little as 10 cents a packet. Most sell 3 or 4 different varieties. These seeds are produced by good companies. However, deeply discounted seed packets do not contain as many seeds as the packs sold at the list price. Our personal experience with the quality of deeply discounted lettuce seeds is satisfactory.

If you have a very small garden or want to enjoy eating home-grown lettuce early, buy 1 or 2 packs of seedlings from a local garden center or nursery. Most sell Black Seeded Simpson, Red Leaf, Green Leaf, and Romaine varieties in packs containing up to 18 seedlings each. Some supermarkets sell lettuce seedlings cheaper than nurseries and garden centers, but the quality is not as good.

To use your garden efficiently, plant lettuce in the area where you plan to grow tomatoes, peppers, and eggplants. By the time these plants grow big, the lettuce will be ready for harvest. We recommend that you give preference to leafy varieties. They are easier to grow, tastier, and contain more vitamins than head varieties. Based on our experience, the easiest lettuce to grow from seeds is Black Seeded Simpson, and the most bolt resistant is Oakleaf.

Preparing the Soil for Lettuce

The Conventional Method: A week before sowing the seeds, work some organic material such as peat moss, humus, or dehydrated manure into the top 4 inches of the soil at the rate of 4 pounds per 10 square feet. Double this rate if the soil is hard, or if the plot was not used to grow vegetables before.

Next, sprinkle a nitrogen-rich fertilizer all over the entire garden at the rate of one cup per 10 square feet. We recommend a fertilizer mix consisting of one part 10-10-10 fertilizer and one part lawn fertilizer. Do not use a lawn fertilizer that contains a weed killer or insecticide. If a lawn fertilizer is not available, use 1 1/2 cups of 10-10-10 alone. Water generously twice before sowing the seeds. Dry chemical fertilizer inhibits seed germination.

Theresa's Alternative Method: In the area you designate for growing lettuce, dig trenches 5 inches wide, 5 inches deep, and 12 inches apart or 5-inch-square holes that are 5 inches deep and 12 inches apart. Prepare potting soil by mixing one part by volume clean topsoil, one part peat moss, and one part dehydrated manure. Add 1/2 cup of 10-10-10 fertilizer and 1/2 cup of lawn fertilizer to each cubic foot of the potting soil and mix well. Do not use lawn fertilizer that contains a weed killer or insecticide. If you don't have lawn fertilizer readily available, use 1 1/2 cups of 10-10-10 fertilizer. Fill the trenches and holes with the mix and water thoroughly.

If you plan to grow lettuce in containers, replace the dehydrated manure with one part perlite or vermiculite and add one cup of bone meal to each cubic foot of the mix.

116

Planting Lettuce

In the conventional method, plant lettuce in rows 12 inches apart. In Theresa's alternative method, plant lettuce in the trenches and holes you filled with potting soil. In both methods, sow the seeds 1/2 inch apart in the rows and trenches or 4 seeds in each hole. Cover the seeds with 1/8 to 1/4 inch soil. Firm the soil over the seeds with the back of a steel rake. Water lightly at least once a day until the seeds germinate.

You can grow lettuce seedlings indoors in containers of any shape or size. Ordinary pots and empty flats that you can get free from nurseries and garden centers may be used. Fill the containers with good potting soil and fertilizer as explained above. Water thoroughly for a few days. Next, sow the seeds in rows or at random. Be generous. Don't worry about the costs of the seeds or that the seedlings will be crowded. Lettuce seedlings transplant well. Cover the seeds with 1/8 to 1/4 inch of potting soil. Next, firm the soil over the seeds. Water lightly once or twice a day until the seeds germinate.

You can grow lettuce seedlings indoors in containers of any shape or size.

When the seedlings grow 4 or more leaves, it is time to transplant them in the garden. Water the seedlings an hour before transplanting in order to reduce the chances of their dehydration. It is very important that you transplant lettuce on a cloudy day or after sunset. Do not transplant lettuce if the following day is forecast to be sunny and hot.

Use a plastic fork or knife to remove as few seedlings as possible in one scoop. Separate the seedlings, making sure not to break the roots. The roots may become bare, but it doesn't matter as long as they are intact. Transplant one seedling every 12 inches in the rows or trenches and one seedling in each hole. Firm the soil around the seedlings, then water generously. In the following few days, the seedlings are likely to dehydrate during their exposure to the sun, but will recover during the night. It is important that you water them frequently, twice a day if possible. When the seedlings grow to the extent that they touch each other, harvest every second one and leave the rest to grow and fill the space in between.

It is recommended that you get as much soil as possible around the roots.

Transplanting lettuce seedlings you buy is very easy, especially if they are grown in separate cells. One hour before transplanting, water the seedlings generously. Remove the seedlings with all the soil around their roots.

Transplant one seedling every 12 inches in the rows or trenches or one in each hole.

Caring for Lettuce

Water the lettuce daily, especially when the weather starts to become hot. After a heavy rain, skip watering for 1 or 2 days. When the seedlings start to touch each other, thin them as explained above. Keep only one seedling in each hole. Fertilize the lettuce every 4 weeks with a nitrogen-rich fertilizer as described above at the rate one cup per 15 plants. Don't let the fertilizer touch the leaves, because it burns them.

When the weather starts to get hot, cover the soil around the lettuce with an organic mulch. Black plastic is not recommended because it makes the soil hotter.

Weeds are not a big problem for lettuce early in the season when the weather is cool. When the weather becomes warm, the weeds grow fast, and unless you cut or cultivate them while small, they will compete with lettuce for food and sunlight.

Watch for diseases and insects, especially aphids. Pull out and discard any diseased plants. If you see aphids, wash the top and bottom sides of the leaves with a water hose. If they persist, add soap to the water. We do not recommend that you use chemical insecticides to kill aphids.

Harvesting Lettuce

Lettuce can be eaten at different stages of growth. When lettuce is small, a person can eat 2 in one sitting. When the weather starts to warm up, lettuce grows quickly. For the best taste and flavor, cut and wash the lettuce immediately before eating it. If you see aphids or other insects in the lettuce, soak the leaves for 5 minutes in a solution consisting of one gallon (about 4 liters) of water, one tablespoon vinegar, and one teaspoon table salt. Home-grown lettuce does not store well in the refrigerator (2 days at the most). Therefore, cut only what you can eat. If you have a bumper crop, and we hope you do, give some to your neighbors and friends or to a soup kitchen, if one is nearby.

Lettuce Diseases

The diseases that attack lettuce include aster yellows, white mold, downy mildew, powdery mildew, bacterial rot, mosaic virus, anthracnose, nematodes, and bacterial wilt.

Lettuce Insects

Aphids are the most common lettuce pests. Other insects include slugs, cabbage loopers, earwigs, leaf miners, spider mites, and whiteflies.

Lettuce Varieties

Lettuce is divided into 4 groups. They are:

1. Looseleaf: Looseleaf varieties includes Black Seeded Simpson, Salad Bowl, Grand Rapids, Royal Oakleaf, and Red Sails.

2. Crisphead: Crisphead, also called Head, varieties includes Iceberg, Summertime, and Ithaca (disease resistant).

3. Cos or Romaine: Cos varieties includes Valmaine, Olga, and Sierra.

4. Butterhead or Boston: Butterhead varieties includes Buttercrunch (heat tolerant), Sangria, Esmeralda, and Little Gem.

Nutritive Value of Lettuce

Lettuce is rich in vitamins A and C and in calcium, potassium, phosphorous, iron, and fiber. Looseleaf, cos, and butterhead have 3 times more calcium and vitamin A and 5 times more vitamin C and iron than crisphead lettuce. Looseleaf contains 5 calories per ounce, while crisphead contains 3.6 calories per ounce. Therefore, no matter how much lettuce you eat, you will not gain weight.

Chapter 12

Spinach

Spinach ought to be grown by every gardener, because it is nutritious, easy to grow, and versatile. When young, the leaves are tender and tasty. They are delicious when eaten raw in salads. Several years ago, we attended a banquet in a luxurious hotel in midtown Manhattan where the salad dish included young spinach leaves. It was so tasty that we decided to add spinach leaves to our salad throughout the harvest season. We also add chopped spinach leaves to omelets. Every one of our guests who have tasted our spinach omelet gives it high marks. Spinach can also be eaten cooked and in stews.

Time to Plant Spinach

In cool areas like the northern United States and Canada, the time to sow spinach seeds in the garden is early spring as soon as the soil can be worked. In areas that don't freeze, like the South and Pacific West, spinach may be sown in the fall for winter harvest and in winter for spring harvest. To extend the harvest season, make successive plantings every 2 weeks but stop when the weather becomes warm, because the seeds will not germinate.

General Information Concerning Spinach

Growing spinach is very much similar to growing lettuce. However, they differ in that spinach plants require less spacing and their roots are deeper compared with lettuce.

You may grow spinach from seeds you sow directly in the garden, from seedlings you grow indoors, or from seedlings you buy.

There is a spinach variety called *New Zealand* that is not a true spinach but it tastes like spinach when cooked. Its advantage is that it resists heat better than ordinary spinach. Similar to ordinary spinach, the seeds of New Zealand spinach must be sown when the weather is cool.

Spinach seeds are bigger than lettuce seeds. They are sold in nurseries, garden centers, and seed catalogs. Some seed catalogs offer trial-size packets containing 50 seeds for a lesser price. You can also buy spinach seeds at a deep discount from several national and local discount stores. Some sell them for as little as 10 cents per packet, but they contain fewer seeds than regular packets. The varieties at these stores are limited, but the quality of the seeds is good. To be on the safe side, buy seeds from different sources. If the seeds of one source don't germinate well, the others will. When buying spinach seeds at full price, choose bolt- and disease-resistant varieties.

Spinach seedlings are sold in nurseries and garden centers in different-size packs. They are expensive but ought to be considered if you want to eat home-grown tender spinach 2 to 3 weeks earlier or if you have a small garden and don't want to bother with growing spinach from seeds.

To use your garden efficiently, plant spinach in the area where you plan to

Spinach seedlings are sold in nurseries and garden centers in different-sizes.

grow tomatoes, peppers, and eggplants. By the time these plants grow big, the spinach will be ready for harvest.

Preparing the Soil for Spinach

The Conventional Method: A week before sowing the seeds, work some organic material such as peat moss, humus, or dehydrated manure into the top 6 inches of the soil at the rate of 4 pounds per 10 square feet. Double this rate if the soil is hard or was not used for growing vegetables before.

Next, sprinkle a nitrogen-rich fertilizer all over the entire area at the rate of one cup per 10 square feet. Nitrogen-rich fertilizer is obtained by mixing one part of 10-10-10 fertilizer with one part lawn fertilizer. Do not use a lawn fertilizer that contains a weed killer or insecticide. If a lawn fertilizer is not readily available, use 1 1/2 cups of 10-10-10 only. Water generously twice before sowing the seeds in order to dilute the concentration of the fertilizer.

Theresa's Alternative Method: In the area in which you plan to grow spinach, dig 4-inch-wide and 6-inch-deep trenches 10 inches apart or 4-inch-square and 6-inch-deep holes that are 10 inches apart. Prepare potting soil by mixing one part by volume clean topsoil, one part peat moss, and one part dehydrated manure. Add one cup of nitrogen-rich fertilizer, as explained earlier, to each cubic foot of the potting soil. Mix well. Fill the trenches and holes with the mix and water thoroughly.

If you plan to grow spinach in containers, replace the dehydrated manure with one part perlite or vermiculite and add one cup bone meal to each cubic foot of the mix.

Planting Spinach

In the conventional method, plant spinach in rows 10 inches apart. In Theresa's alternative method, plant spinach in the trenches and holes you filled with potting soil. In both methods, sow the seeds 1 inch apart in the rows and trenches or 4 seeds in each hole. Cover the seeds with 1/4 inch of soil. Firm the soil with the back of a steel rake. Water lightly once or twice a day until the seeds germinate.

For early harvest, grow spinach seedlings indoors. Four to 6 weeks before the date of last frost, fill a container or pots with potting soil and fertilizer as described above in Theresa's alternative method. Water thoroughly for a couple of days. Next, sow the seeds in rows or at random. Be generous with the seeds, especially if you have bought them at deep discount. Cover the seeds with 1/8 to 1/4 inch of potting soil. Next, firm the soil over the seeds. Water lightly once or twice a day until the seeds germinate.

When the seedlings grow 4 or more leaves, it is time to transplant them in the garden. One hour before transplanting, water the seedlings so that the leaves absorb as much water as possible. This reduces the chances of their dehydration after transplanting. It is also important that you do the transplanting on cloudy days or after sunset. Do not transplant spinach if the following day is forecast to be hot and sunny. Use a plastic knife to separate the seedlings but be careful not to break their roots. Transplant one seedling every 10 inches in the rows and trenches or one in each hole. Firm the soil around the seedlings, then water generously. Keep some

For early harvest, grow spinach seedlings indoors.

seedlings in reserve. If some seedlings don't make it, transplant others in their places.

Transplanting bought spinach seedlings is the easiest, because they are relatively big, with ample soil around their roots. It is important that you transplant the seedlings shortly after buying them. One hour before trans-planting, water the seedlings generously for the reasons described above. If there are more than one seedling in each cell, separate them carefully in order not to break the roots. Transplant a seedling every 10 inches in the row or trench or one in each hole. Water immediately after transplanting.

Caring for Spinach

For vigorous growth, spinach should be watered daily. If the plants grown from seeds sown directly in the garden start to touch each other, thin them to 10 inches apart. Fertilize the spinach every 4 weeks with nitrogen-rich fertilizer as described above at the rate of one cup per 15 plants. Do not let the fertilizer touch the leaves, because it will burn them.

When the weather starts to become hot, cover the soil around spinach plants with organic mulch. Do not use black plastic mulch, because it makes the soil hotter.

Weeds are not a problem early in the season, but when the weather warms up, they grow fast. They should be cultivated while still small and when the soil is moist. Be careful not to disturb the plant roots.

Watch for diseases and insects. Pick and discard the insects and infected plants. If aphids appear, wash both sides of the leaves with a water hose. If this doesn't work, add soap to the water. We don't recommend the use of chemical pesticides on spinach. The health risk and high cost of the pesticides don't justify their use.

Harvesting Spinach

When the plants grow several leaves, start harvesting them. Either pick the big outer leaves from each plant and let the rest grow, or cut every second plant to make room for the rest to grow. It is important that you wash the leaves thoroughly before eating them raw or cooked. If you see any aphids or other insects, soak the spinach for 5 minutes in a solution consisting of one gallon (about 4 liters) of water, one tablespoon vinegar, and one teaspoon table salt, then rinse thoroughly.

Home-grown spinach is tender and delicate. It doesn't store well in the refrigerator (3 days at the most). Therefore, harvest only what you can eat fresh.

Spinach Diseases

The most common spinach diseases are downy mildew, leaf mold, verticillium wilt, white rust, anthracnose, root rot, and cucumber mosaic.

Spinach Insects

The insects that attack spinach include spinach leaf miners, cabbage loopers, flea beetles, spider mites, and aphids.

Spinach Varieties

Spinach varieties include Olympia (resists mildew), Vienna, Melody, Bloomsdale Long Standing (slow bolting), Green Giant (disease resistant), Medania (disease resistant), Noble Giant, Correnta, Avon, and Tyee.

Nutritive Value of Spinach

Spinach is very rich in vitamins A and B_2 and in iron and calcium. It also contains vitamin C, potassium, and phosphorous. One ounce of raw spinach contains only 5.5 calories.

Recipe for Low-Cholesterol Spinach Omelet

We love omelets. We are also conscious about our cholesterol. The USDA recommended daily cholesterol intake is 300 milligrams, which is the amount contained in one egg yolk. Therefore, we use only one yolk in our omelet and discard the rest. Adding fresh garden spinach to the omelet makes it tasty and nutritious.

Ingredients for 2 Servings

4 large eggs
1 cup chopped garden spinach
salt and black pepper to taste
1/2 tablespoon butter
1 tablespoon olive or vegetable oil

Cooking Directions

Break the 4 eggs. Discard the yolks of 3 eggs and leave the yolk of only one egg. Beat the eggs. Add the chopped spinach, salt, and pepper and mix. Meanwhile, heat the butter and oil in a skillet over moderate heat. Pour the egg-spinach mix into the skillet for a couple of minutes until the bottom becomes golden. Flip the omelet onto the other side and cook for one more minute. Serve hot and enjoy this delicious and nutritious meal.

Chapter 13

Peas

Peas are not easy for beginners to grow. However, you can grow peas successfully if you know the conditions under which they thrive. These conditions are (1) limed light soil that is rich in phosphorous, potassium, and organic matter, (2) full sun, and (3) cool days and cooler nights.

Time to Plant Peas

In cool areas like the northern United States and Canada, peas should be sown in early spring as soon as the soil can be worked. In areas that don't freeze, like the South and Pacific West, peas may be sown in spring or fall. To extend the harvest season, make successive plantings every 2 weeks but stop when the weather warms up, because pea seeds will not germinate.

General Information Concerning Peas

There are 3 pea varieties: (1) snow peas, (2) snap or sugar peas, and (3) green peas, also called garden peas or English peas.

Snow peas are eaten whole, peas and pods. However, they should be picked at the time when the pods are still flat. Snow peas mature in 6 to 8 weeks.

Snow peas are expensive to buy. Nearby supermarkets sell them for up to $4 a pound. Most of the time they are not fresh, because they stay on the shelves for several days. Snow peas lose their flavor and nutritive value quickly. Therefore, they should be cooked shortly after picking. We cook the snow peas with their flowers still attached to them.

Snow peas are an important ingredient in Chinese cooking. We love Chinese food, but find restaurants' cooking greasy. Therefore, we developed a lighter version of Chinese chicken breast with home-grown snow peas. The recipe for this delicious dish is given at the end of this chapter.

Snap or sugar peas are so sweet that they may be eaten raw. They can be cooked whole when picked before their pods are fully developed. When the pods develop fully, they should be shelled before cooking. Snap peas mature in 9 to 10 weeks.

Green peas should be shelled before cooking. They are available in dwarf and pole varieties. The pole varieties take a longer time to mature but yield more. Garden peas mature in 10 to 12 weeks.

Peas do not need much nitrogen because they are legumes. Legumes have special bacteria attached to their roots that absorb nitrogen from the air and fix it on the plants' roots in a soluble form. If you fertilize the peas with a fertilizer that contains too much nitrogen, the plants produce big leaves and small pods.

Peas should be grown from seeds. Pea seeds may be bought from seed catalogs, nurseries, garden centers, supermarkets, and discount stores. Some seed catalogs offer trial-size packets containing 75 seeds for a fraction of the price of the standard packet. The deeply discounted seed packets contain far fewer seeds than the packets offered by seed catalogs. The variety is limited but the quality is good. If you want a specific variety, you have to buy it from a seed catalog. Choose varieties that are disease resistant and heat tolerant. Read the information on the package or in the seed catalog before buying.

Preparing the Soil for Peas

The Conventional Method: A week before sowing the seeds, work some organic material such as peat moss or humus into the top 6 inches of the soil at the rate of 4 pounds per 10 square feet. Double this rate if the soil is hard, or if the plot was not used to grow vegetables before. Add lime at the rate of one cup per 15 square feet. Next, apply a low-nitrogen fertilizer such as 5-10-10 at the rate of one cup per 15 square feet. Mix well, then water thoroughly before sowing the seeds.

Theresa's Alternative Method: In the area you allocate for growing peas, dig circular trenches 6 inches wide, 6 inches deep, and 15 inches in diameter. The reason for digging circular trenches is to use tomato cages to support the peas. This is easier than planting in straight rows and erecting trestles for support.

Prepare potting soil by mixing one part clean topsoil and one part peat moss. Add one cup of 5-10-10 fertilizer and 3/4 cup lime to each cubic foot of potting soil and mix well. Fill the trenches with the mix and water thoroughly.

If you plan to grow peas in containers, add 1/2 cubic foot perlite or vermiculite and one cup bone meal to each cubic foot of the mix.

Planting Peas

In the conventional method, plant peas in single rows 12 inches apart or in double rows 16 inches apart. Sow pea seeds one inch deep and 2 inches apart in both directions. Double rows utilize the land better, reduce watering, keep the plants cool, and reduce the need for support. One trestle support both rows. In Theresa's alternative method, plant peas in double rows in the circular trenches that have been filled with potting soil. Sow the seeds one inch deep and 2 inches apart in both directions. Use tomato cages to support the plants. In both methods, firm the soil over the seeds with the back of a steel rake. Water lightly once or twice a day until the seeds germinate.

Peas grow well in containers. Your first choice should be snow peas, because they are expensive to buy and the plants are small. Your second choice should be dwarf varieties of sugar peas. Your third choice should be dwarf garden peas.

We don't recommend that you plant peas from seedlings grown indoors or bought. Peas don't transplant well. If out of curiosity or for the sake of fun, you decide to grow peas from seedlings you buy, water them well an hour before transplanting. Next, transplant them 2 inches apart in rows or circles as described above.

Caring for Peas

Peas need daily watering. When the plants are 4 inches tall, feed them with a 5-10-10 fertilizer at the rate of one cup per 20 feet of single rows or 10 feet of double rows. Peas are light feeders. Therefore, don't fertilize them any more. When the pole peas are 6 inches tall, train them onto the supports. Don't walk very close to the plants in order not to compact the soil around the roots. This is particularly important when the soil is wet. Also, watch for insects and diseases.

Harvesting Peas

Snow peas should be picked when the peas inside the pods start to develop. If you wait too long, the pods will swell and the peas become tough. Sugar peas should be picked when the peas are developed, but before the pod's green shiny color starts to fade. Green peas should be picked when the peas are swollen and the pods are shiny green. Don't wait until the pods become tough and lose their shine. With time and practice you will become an expert in picking the peas at the peak of ripeness.

Pick the peas frequently to ensure quality and promote productivity. Pinch the neck of the pods from the plants or cut them with scissors in order not to damage the vines. The best time to harvest peas is in the morning when the pods are crisp. Ideally, you should cook the peas shortly after they are picked. Put what is left in the refrigerator. If the peas are kept in warm air for a few hours, they lose their sweetness. This explains why the peas sold in the market are tough and tasteless. You will know the difference after you taste the peas you grow.

Pea Diseases

The most common diseases that attack peas are downy mildew, powdery mildew, root rot, leaf spots, mosaic virus, scab, fusarium wilt, bacterial blight, anthracnose, and nematodes.

Pea Insects

The most common pea insects are the aphids, pea weevils, pea moths, leaf miners, cucumber beetles, seed corn maggots, cabbage loopers, and whiteflies.

Pea Varieties

Snow Peas: Snow pea varieties include Oregon Sugar Pod (disease resistant), Dwarf Gray Sugar, Dwarf White Sugar, Mammoth Melting Sugar (resists wilt), Snow Green (resists powdery mildew), and Snowflake (resists wilt and powdery mildew).

Snap Peas: Snap pea varieties include Sugar Snap (resists wilt), Super Sugar Snap (resists mildew), Sugar Ann (disease resistant), Sugar Lace, Sugar Bon, and Sugar Daddy.

Green Peas: Green pea varieties include Little Marvel, Lincoln (resists wilt), Green Arrow (resists wilt and mildew), Laxton's Progress, Wando (resists heat), Payload, and Maestro (resists heat and mildew).

Nutritive Value of Peas

Peas are rich in potassium, phosphorous, and vitamins A, B, and C. Cooked green peas contain 20 calories per ounce. Cooked snow and snap peas contain 11.5 calories per ounce.

Recipe for Chicken Breast with Snow Peas, Chinese Style

This is a light and tasty meal that takes only 20 minutes to prepare and costs about $2 per serving. The snow peas we grow in containers and a little space in the garden give us enough harvest to feast on this meal from the end of May until the middle of July. We also like to cook it for our close friends. It makes a nice piece of conversation. We get a kick out of it when they tell us how delicious and light the meal is and how little time and effort it takes to prepare.

Ingredients for 4 Servings

4 cups boiled or fried rice
1 tablespoon butter
3 tablespoons olive or vegetable oil
2 chicken breasts, diced
4 slices (1/4-inch thick) of a large onion, quartered
2 tablespoons soy or teriyaki sauce
4 cups fresh home-grown snow peas
2 ounces cashews or shelled almonds (optional)

Cooking Directions

Start by cooking the rice because it takes the longest time. Put one cup of dry white rice in a pan. Add 2 cups of water, one chicken bouillon cube, and 1/2 tablespoon butter and one tablespoon olive oil (delete the butter and olive oil if you want boiled rice). Bring to boil while stirring to dissolve the chicken bouillon cube. Cover the pan and lower the heat to warm. After about 20 minutes, the rice will be done. Turn off the heat.

While the rice is cooking, add the butter and oil to a skillet and set the heat on medium-high. When the butter and oil become hot, add the diced chicken breast and the onion to the skillet. Stir continuously until the chicken is cooked (6-8 minutes). Add the soy or teriyaki sauce, the snow peas, and cashews or almonds (optional). Stir for an additional 2 minutes. Your meal is done. Lower the heat to warm until the rice is cooked, then turn off the heat. Put the chicken on one side of each dish and the rice on the other side. Serve immediately and enjoy.

Chicken breast with snow peas, Chinese style.

Chapter 14

Cabbage

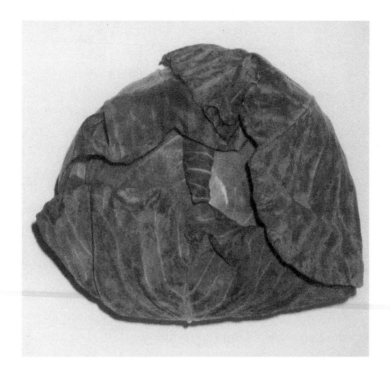

Cabbage needs fertile soil. It is easy to grow from seeds. It tolerates frost but is sensitive to heat. Cabbage is versatile. It can be made into coleslaw and sauerkraut. The leaves may be boiled, steamed, or stuffed with rice and ground meat. The latter is a delicacy in Middle Eastern cooking.

Time to Plant Cabbage

In cool areas like the northern United States and Canada, cabbage seeds may be sown throughout the spring, the earlier the better. In areas that don't freeze, like the South and Pacific West, seeds may be sown in late fall for winter harvest and in early winter for a spring harvest. To extend the harvest season, make successive plantings every 2 weeks.

General Information Concerning Cabbage

Cabbage grows best when day temperatures are 70° to 80° F (21.1° to 26.7° C) and night temperatures are 50° to 60° F (10° to 15.6° C). If the temperature stays cooler or warmer than these temperatures for an extended period of time, the cabbage will not form a big head and instead may bolt (form seeds). If hot weather persists, the head splits.

To reduce the chances of disease, don't grow cabbage in a spot where cabbage or any other cole crop (broccoli, brussels sprouts, cauliflower, and kohlrabi) had been grown in the previous year.

Cabbage may be grown from seeds sown directly in the garden, from seedlings grown indoors, or from seedlings you buy.

Cabbage seeds may be bought from nurseries, garden centers, seed catalogs or discount stores. Seed catalogs offer packets containing 100 to 250 seeds. The price varies, depending on the variety.

Discount stores offer limited varieties at deep discount. The quality of the seeds is good. However, the number of seeds per packet is lower than in the packets sold by seed catalogs.

If you have a small garden and want to grow only a few plants, buy a pack of seedlings from a nursery or garden center. Big nurseries sell at least 3 varieties. When buying cabbage seedlings, choose ones having short, thick stems and big, shiny leaves. Also, choose disease-resistant varieties.

Preparing the Soil for Cabbage

The Conventional Method: A week before planting, work some organic material such as peat moss, humus, dehydrated manure, or composted manure into the top 6 inches of the soil at the rate of 4 pounds per 10 square feet. Double this rate if the soil is hard or if the plot was not used to grow vegetables before. Next, sprinkle 10-10-10 fertilizer at the rate of one cup per 10 square feet. Water thoroughly.

Theresa's Alternative Method: In the area you designate for growing cabbage, dig one-foot-square holes 8 inches deep and 1 1/2 feet apart. Prepare potting soil by mixing one part by volume clean topsoil, one part peat moss, and one part dehydrated manure. Additionally, add one cup of 10-10-10 fertilizer to each cubic foot of the potting soil. Mix well, then water thoroughly.

If you plan to grow cabbage in containers, replace the dehydrated manure with one part perlite or vermiculite and add one cup of bone meal to each cubic foot of the mix.

Planting Cabbage

In the conventional method, plant cabbage in rows 1 1/2 feet apart. If growing from seeds sown directly in the garden, sow the seeds one inch apart and 1/4 inch deep. Firm the soil over the seeds with the back of a steel rake. If you grow from seedlings, transplant one seedling every 1 1/2 feet.

In Theresa's alternative method, sow 4 or 5 seeds in the middle of each hole that you filled with potting soil and cover with 1/4 inch soil. Water lightly once or twice a day until the seeds germinate. When the seedlings grow 3 inches high, leave the strongest seedling and cut or transplant the rest. If you grow from seedlings, transplant one seedling in the middle of each hole, then fill around it. Firm the soil over the seeds and around the seedlings.

For early harvest, grow cabbage seedlings indoors. Fill a container or pots with potting soil as explained in Theresa's alternative method. Next, sow the seeds in rows or at random. Cover the seeds with 1/4 inch potting soil.

Firm the soil over the seeds, then water lightly once or twice a day until the seeds germinate.

Caring for Cabbage

It is important that you keep the weeds under control until the cabbage grows big. Mulch around the plants with organic mulch. When the weather is cool, weeds are not a problem. As the weather warms up, weeds emerge through the mulch. Yank the weeds while small and add more mulch in the bare areas to prevent weeds from spreading. Water regularly but don't overwater the cabbage because this causes the heads to split. When the seedlings grown from seeds sown directly in the garden are close to each other, thin them to 1 1/2 feet apart.

Feed the cabbage every month with a 10-10-10 fertilizer at the rate of one cup per 4 plants. Watch for diseases and insects. Pull out and discard diseased plants. Avoid touching the plants when they are wet. If the insects are few, pick and destroy them. If there are too many, take a sample to a big nursery. The staff will identify the insects and recommend an insecticide that kills them.

Harvesting Cabbage

Start harvesting cabbage when the heads are about 6 inches (15 centimeters) across. Cut the head with a sharp knife and discard the rest of the plant. Cabbage can be harvested throughout the season. Cook what you need and refrigerate the rest. Cabbage refrigerates well for 1 to 2 weeks.

Cabbage Diseases

Cabbage diseases include black rot, leaf spots, club root, downy mildew, powdery mildew, white rust, and nematodes.

Cabbage Insects

The main insects that attack cabbage are cabbage maggots, imported cabbageworms, cabbage loopers, aphids, cutworms, and cabbage flea beetles.

Cabbage Varieties

Green: Green varieties include Stonehead, Late Flat Dutch, Golden Cross, Green Jewels, Savoy Express, Tropic Giant, Augusta, and Copenhagen Market.

Red: Red varieties include Raven, Red Dynasty, Red Jewel, and Super Red.

Nutritive Value of Cabbage

Cabbage has moderate amounts of vitamins A and C and of potassium, calcium, sulfur, and phosphorous. One ounce of cabbage contains 6.1 calories.

Chapter 15

Potatoes

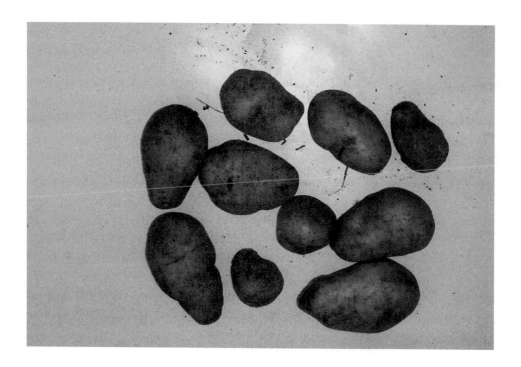

You should consider growing some potatoes, especially if you have a big garden. In addition to being easy to grow, it is fun to uncover the earth and find potato clusters waiting to be picked. One of the advantages of growing potatoes is that you can pick them small, when they taste best. You won't find this quality in the market. Potatoes can be boiled, baked, grilled, made into French fries, or added to soups and stews. Potatoes come in different colors: white, red, yellow, and blue!

Time to Plant Potatoes

In cool areas like the northern United States and Canada, start planting potatoes 4 weeks before the last frost. In areas that don't freeze, like the South and Pacific West, start planting potatoes in January for early summer harvest and in early September for winter harvest.

General Information Concerning Potatoes

A potato plant consists of a green vine that grows above ground and a cluster of potatoes, called *tubers*, that grow below the surface.

Potatoes are grown from seeds, also called *sets*. Potato seeds are not actual seeds. Rather, they are pieces of a big potato or whole small ones. Each piece must contain at least one eye. An eye is a dormant bud that sprouts into a potato plant. Most of the potatoes sold in the market are chemically treated to inhibit sprouting of the eyes. These cannot be used

Some of the potatoes you buy in the market may sprout. These can be cut and used as seeds.

to grow potatoes. However, some of the potatoes you buy in the market may sprout, which indicates that they have not been treated. These can be cut and used as seeds if you plan to grow only a few plants for fun. However, you should inspect the potatoes carefully to ensure that they are not diseased.

Each seed should be about a one-inch cube and contain one or more eyes. Big seeds produce many small tubers, while small seeds produce a few big tubers. After cutting the seeds, leave them in a humid place for 2 days before planting. This cures them and prevents their rot when planted. You may also dust the seeds with sulfur powder, which you can buy at some nurseries.

If you plan to grow many plants, you are better off buying sets from a seed catalog. Catalog sets are treated to kill surface fungus and bacteria.

Potatoes are subject to several diseases and viruses. Therefore, it is important that you buy disease-resistant varieties. Seed catalogs indicate the diseases each variety resists.

Potatoes require fertile, light, and acidic soil. Light soil allows the tubers to grow with little resistance. It also drains well, which prevents tuber rot. Acidic soil inhibits potato scab, a fungus that infects the skin of the potatoes.

You should rotate the potatoes—don't plant them in the same spot 2 years in a row. This reduces the chances of infecting them with diseases and insects that winter in the soil.

Some potato varieties are classified as early, midseason, and late season. This refers to the time in which they reach maturity. Early potatoes mature sooner than midseason potatoes if they are planted at the same time. If you live in a cool area, choose early varieties.

Preparing the Soil for Potatoes

The Conventional Method: Two weeks before sowing the seeds, work some organic material such as peat moss or humus into the top 10 inches of the soil at the rate of 8 pounds per 10 square feet.

Potatoes may be planted in *trenches* or *hills.* In the former, dig trenches that are 6 inches wide and 10 inches deep, spaced 3 feet apart. After digging the trenches, mix the dug-up soil with 5-10-10 fertilizer at the rate of one cup per 5 feet. Fill 5 inches of the trenches with half the dug-up soil and water thoroughly.

To plant in hills, dig holes that are 3 feet square and 5 inches deep, 4 feet apart. Mix the dug-up soil with 5-10-10 fertilizer at the rate of one cup per hill. Fill the holes with the dug-up soil and water thoroughly. (At this stage, the top of the filled holes will be level with the rest of the garden.)

Theresa's Alternative Method: In the area you allocate for growing potatoes, dig 3-foot-square and 10-inch-deep holes spaced 4 feet apart. Prepare potting soil by mixing one part by volume clean topsoil and one part peat moss. Add one cup 5-10-10 fertilizer to each cubic foot of potting soil. Fill 5 inches of the holes with the mix. Water thoroughly.

Planting Potatoes

In the conventional method, if you are planting in trenches, sow potato seeds 6 inches apart, then fill the trenches with the rest of the dug-up soil. Water thoroughly. If you are planting in hills, place 4 potato seeds in a 6-inch circle at the center of each hill. Cover the seeds with 5 inches of soil. The top of the hills will be 5 inches higher than the rest of the garden. Water thoroughly.

In Theresa's alternative method, place 4 seeds in a 6-inch circle at the center of each hole. Cover the seeds with 5 inches of the potting soil. The top of the hill will be level with the rest of the garden. Sprinkle 1/2 cup all-purpose fertilizer over each hill, then water thoroughly.

Caring for Potatoes

When the vines grow, watch to see if tubers appear above the surface. If they do, cover them immediately by adding more soil. If you don't do that, the above-ground parts of the potatoes will be green. These parts are slightly poisonous and should not be eaten.

About 4 weeks after planting, add 5-10-10 fertilizer at the rate of one cup per 10 feet of trenches or 1/2 cup per hill. When the weather warms up, weeds will be a problem. Cut them early, while they are still small. Watch for insects and diseases. If insects are few, pick them by hand (always wear gloves) and destroy them. If there are many, take a sample to a near-by big nursery. The staff will give you an insecticide. The best defense against diseases is to choose disease-resistant varieties.

Harvesting Potatoes

When the vines start to turn yellow, dig up the tubers and pick what you need, then cover the rest. Be careful not to damage the tubers. When the vines dry up, the tubers stop growing.

After digging the potatoes, leave them outdoors for a couple of hours to dry up. Store them in a cool place or in the refrigerator. Potatoes can be stored for weeks.

It is possible that you may unintentionally leave some tubers in the ground. These will become seeds and grow the following year. You will be surprised to see potato vines growing out of nowhere!

Potato Diseases

Potatoes are susceptible to several diseases including potato scab, early and late blight, powdery mildew, verticillium wilt, fusarium wilt, anthrac-nose, and nematodes.

Potato Insects

Potato insects include Colorado potato beetles, flea beetles, wireworms, European corn borers, leafhoppers, leaf miners, corn earworms, tomato hornworms, and nematodes (nematodes are both diseases and insects).

Potato Varieties

Potato varieties include Russet Burbank (baking, disease resistant),

Norgold Russet (early to midseason), Beltsville (disease resistant, midseason), Frontier, White Cobbler, Kennebec (late season), Norland (red), Red Pontiac (early season), All Blue (blue), and Yukon Gold (yellow).

Nutritive Value of Potatoes

Potatoes are rich in potassium, phosphorous, and niacin (vitamin B_3). Baked potatoes contain 31 calories per ounce and boiled potatoes 26 calories per ounce. Potatoes are an inexpensive source of carbohydrates.

Chapter 16

Broccoli

Broccoli is gaining popularity because several medical studies indicate that it protects our body against cancer. Broccoli may be eaten raw, steamed, boiled, or stir-fried.

Time to Plant Broccoli

In cool areas like the northern United States and Canada, broccoli should be planted as soon as the soil can be worked so that it can be harvested before hot weather arrives. In warm areas like the South, broccoli can be planted in late fall for a winter crop or in winter for a spring crop. To extend the harvest season, make successive plantings every 2 weeks before the weather becomes warm.

General Information Concerning Broccoli

Broccoli is a member of the cole or cabbage family. The edible head is a cluster of small flowers (florets) that are in bud form. If not harvested at the proper time, the buds bloom into yellow flowers and become inedible. To reduce the chances of disease, broccoli should not be planted in the spot where broccoli or any other cole crop has been grown in the previous 2 years.

Broccoli grows best when the day temperature is 70° F (21.1° C) and the night temperature is about 50° F (10° C). It may be grown from seeds sown directly in the garden or from seedlings grown indoors or bought. Seeds may be bought from nurseries, garden centers, seed catalogs, or discount stores. Seed catalogs offer the biggest variety. They sell packets containing 150 to 200 seeds for a price that varies, depending on the variety. Discount stores offer the least variety and the number of seeds per packet is smaller than those in seed catalog packets.

Broccoli germinates best when the day temperature is 75° F (23.9° C) and the night temperature is 55° F (12.8° C). If you grow it indoors in a heated area where the temperature is 70° F (21.1° C) day and night, seedlings will grow leggy, meaning tall, weak stems and small leaves. If you don't have proper heating and lighting equipment for planting, you are better off buying seedlings or sowing seeds directly in the garden.

If your garden is small or if you don't want to grow much broccoli, buy a pack or two of seedlings from a nursery or garden center. Big nurseries offer 2 or 3 varieties. Choose varieties that mature fast and are disease and bolt resistant.

Preparing the Soil for Broccoli

The Conventional Method: A week before planting, work some organic material such as peat moss, humus, or dehydrated manure into the top 6 inches of the soil at the rate of 4 pounds per 10 square feet. Double this rate if the soil is hard or if the plot was not used to grow vegetables before. Next, sprinkle 10-10-10 fertilizer at the rate of one cup per 10 square feet. Water thoroughly.

Theresa's Alternative Method: In the area you designate for broccoli, dig 8-inch-square holes that are 8 inches deep and 18 inches apart. Fill the holes with good potting soil made of one part clean topsoil, one part peat moss, and one part dehydrated manure. Add one cup of 10-10-10 fertilizer to each cubic foot of the potting soil. Mix well and water thoroughly.

If you plan to grow broccoli in containers, replace the dehydrated manure with one part perlite or vermiculite and add one cup bone meal to each cubic foot of the mix.

Planting Broccoli

In the conventional method, plant broccoli in rows 18 inches apart. If you grow from seeds, sow one seed every 2 inches, then cover with 1/2 inch soil. If you grow from seedlings, transplant one seedling every 18 inches. Firm the soil over the seeds and around the seedlings, then water thoroughly.

In Theresa's alternative method, if growing from seeds, sow 3 or 4 seeds in the middle of each hole. Cover the seeds with 1/2 inch soil. When the seedlings grow to 3 inches high, keep the strongest seedlings and pinch or transplant the rest. If growing from seedlings, transplant one seedling in each hole, then fill around it with potting soil. Firm the soil over the seeds and around the seedlings. Water thoroughly.

To get an early start, sow the seeds indoors 4 weeks before they are to be transplanted outdoors. Broccoli roots don't like to be disturbed. Therefore, grow every plant in a separate cell or container. Sow 3 or 4 seeds per cell or container. When they grow to about 3 inches high, leave the strongest seedling and pinch or transplant the rest. This way the plants will have enough room to grow and the roots will not be disturbed when transplanted.

Caring for Broccoli

When growing from seeds sown directly in the soil, keep the strongest seedling in every 18 inches or every hole. Transplant the extras or pinch them if you don't have space for them. Weeds are no problem early in the season when the weather is cool, but they become a problem when the weather warms up. Mulch around the broccoli plants with a thick layer of organic material. Water daily.

Fertilize the broccoli every 4 weeks with a 10-10-10 fertilizer at the rate of 1/4 cup per plant. Watch for diseases and insects. If the infection is light, pull the diseased plants and pick the insects by hand and destroy them (always wear gloves). If the infection is moderate to heavy, take a sample and show it to a nursery's staff or your cooperative extension expert. Both will identify the disease or insect and recommend a pesticide. Read the manufacturer's instructions carefully, particularly with respect to application and the number of days that must pass before harvesting.

Harvesting Broccoli

Harvest the central head when it is big enough and the buds are green and tight. Harvest the heads before the buds open. Use a sharp knife to cut the crown with about 3 inches of the stem. When the smaller side shoots grow big enough, harvest them before their buds open. If the weather is favorable, broccoli plants will keep growing until frost.

Broccoli Diseases

The most common broccoli diseases are black rot, club root, leaf spots, downy mildew, powdery mildew, white rust, and nematodes.

Broccoli Insects

The most common insects that attack broccoli are cabbage aphids, cabbage loopers, imported cabbageworms, cabbage maggots, flea beetles, and nematodes (nematodes are both diseases and insects).

Broccoli Varieties

Broccoli varieties include Green Comet (tolerates heat, resists disease, early producer), Packman, Emperor, Captain, Green Goliath, Super Dome, Small Miracle, Paragon, and Regal.

Nutritive Value of Broccoli

Broccoli is very rich in vitamins A, B_3, and C and rich in potassium, phosphorous, calcium, sulfur, and iron. It contains 7.5 calories per ounce.

Part 3

Hardy Vegetables

Chapters in This Part

Chapter 17

Beets

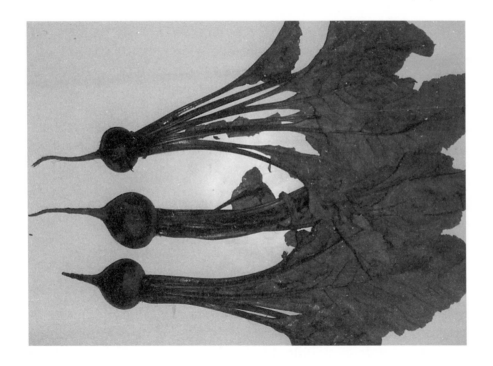

Beets are easy to grow. They prefer cool weather but tolerate mild frost as well as warm weather. They do best in full sun but grow fairly well in partial shade.

Time to Plant Beets

In cool areas like the northern United States and Canada, the seeds can

155

be sown directly in the garden 2 weeks before the last frost. In areas that don't freeze, like the South and Pacific West, start sowing the seeds in early spring for a summer harvest and in the fall for a winter harvest. For continuous harvest, make successive plantings at 2-week intervals.

General Information Concerning Beets

Beets require soil that is moist and rich in phosphorous and potassium. Not all beets are red. The Golden and Albino White varieties do not bleed red when cut. However, their seeds don't germinate as well as the red varieties.

Both the beets' roots and green tops are edible. In fact, the green tops are more nutritious than the roots. They are less messy, too. Both roots and greens can be eaten raw, in green salad, or cooked.

Beet seeds are actually clusters, each containing several seeds. Not all the seeds in a cluster germinate at the same time. As a result, seedlings of different sizes emerge from one cluster.

Beets germinate best when the day temperature is 65° to 70° F (18.3° to 21.1° C) and the night temperature is 55° to 60° F (12.8° to 15.6° C). The soil should be loose, rich in organic matter, and free of rocks. Beets require soil having a pH value of 6.7 to 7.0. This is more alkaline than what most vegetables require.

Beets may be grown from seeds sown directly in the garden, from seedlings you grow indoors, or seedlings you buy. The former is recommended because beets germinate quickly. Beet seeds may be bought from nurseries, garden centers, or discount stores. Seed catalogs sell packets, each containing 400 seeds. Some seed catalogs offer trial-size packets containing 100 seeds for about one-third the price of the standard packet. It is important to use fresh seeds, because the seeds of the previous year will not germinate well. To save money, buy some seeds from discount stores. The variety is limited but the quality is good.

You may buy seedlings from nurseries or garden centers. Seedlings are sold in packs or trays. The price varies depending on where you live.

Preparing the Soil for Beets

The Conventional Method: Two weeks before planting, work some organic material such as peat moss or humus at the rate of 4 pounds per 10 square feet into the top 8 inches of the soil. Next, sprinkle 5-10-10 fertilizer at the rate of one cup per 10 square feet and either lime at the rate of one cup per 20 square feet or wood ashes at the rate of 2 cups per 10 square feet. Water thoroughly.

Do not use raw manure, because it adversely affects the quality and quantity of the beets.

Theresa's Alternative Method: In the area you allocate for beets, dig 5-inch-wide and 8-inch-deep trenches 12 inches apart for single-row planting. For wide-row planting, the trenches should be 14 to 16 inches wide. Prepare potting soil by mixing one part by volume clean topsoil and one part organic material such as peat moss or humus. Add one cup 5-10-10 fertilizer and either one cup of lime or 2 cups of wood ashes to each cubic foot of the potting soil. Fill the trenches with the mix, then water thoroughly a few times before planting. If you grow beets for their green tops, dig 2-foot-wide and 8-inch-deep trenches and fill them with the same potting soil.

If you plan to grow beets in containers, add 1/2 cubic foot perlite or vermiculite and one cup bone meal to each cubic foot of the mix.

Planting Beets

Beet seeds should be sown 1/2 inch deep in cool weather, 3/4 inch deep in warm weather, and 1 inch deep in hot weather. This is to prevent the seeds from drying.

In the conventional method, beets may be planted in single rows 12 inches apart or wide rows 16 inches wide. If you grow beets mainly for their green tops, use wide rows. Sow the seeds one inch apart, whether in single or wide rows. If growing from seedlings, transplant one seedling every 4 inches. After sowing the seeds or transplanting the seedlings, firm the soil, then water thoroughly.

In Theresa's alternative method, sow the seeds one inch apart in the middle of the single-row trench and one inch apart each direction in wide-row trenches. Firm the soil over them, then water thoroughly.

You may grow beet seedlings indoors. Four weeks before the date of last frost, fill 4-inch-deep flats or pots with potting soil as explained above in Theresa's alternative method. Water thoroughly. Next, sow the seeds one inch apart in both directions and cover with 1/4 inch of soil. Water lightly twice a day.

Transplanting seedlings grown indoors or bought is easy. It is preferable to choose a cloudy day or wait until after sunset. Water the seedlings well an hour before transplanting.

Caring for Beets

It is important to keep the area around beets weed free. Pull the weeds as soon as they emerge. Use 4-inch-thick organic mulch. When the seedlings grow to 3 inches high, thin them to 4 inches apart. Eat the nutritious green tops either raw or cooked. Fertilize the beets every month with 5-10-10 fertilizer at the rate of one cup per 10 feet for single rows or per 3 feet for wide rows. Keeping beets moist is essential. Watch for diseases and insects.

Harvesting Beets

Start harvesting the green tops when they reach 5 inches high. Either pull up the entire plant or cut the biggest leaves one inch above the ground with a knife or scissors. This prevents root bleeding. Start harvesting the roots when they reach the size of a golf ball, and harvest when the soil is dry. Beets refrigerate well for a week or more.

Beet Diseases

Beet diseases include bacterial blight, downy mildew, powdery mildew, leaf spots, white rust, black rot, scab, cucumber mosaic, verticillium wilt, and fusarium wilt.

Beet Insects

Beets may be attacked by aphids, leaf miners, cutworms, wireworms, leafhoppers, cabbage loopers, and cabbage maggots.

Beet Varieties

Beet varieties include Detroit Dark Red, Ruby Queen, Baby Gladiator, Red Ace (expensive), Golden (does not bleed red), Pacemaker III (expensive), Perfected Detroit, and Formanova.

Nutritive Value of Beets

Beet roots are rich in potassium, iron, and phosphorous. They contain 9 calories per ounce. Beet greens (leaves and stems) are very rich in vitamins A and C and in potassium and calcium. They contain 6 calories per ounce.

Chapter 18

Carrots

C arrots are very rich in vitamin A. One ounce of raw carrots contains all your body's need for vitamin A for one day. Carrots grow in cool as well as warm weather but don't take frost well.

Time to Plant Carrots

In cool areas like the northern United States and Canada, carrot seeds may be sown directly in the ground from mid spring to midsummer. Because carrots tolerate heat, they can be planted throughout the season until 60 days before the first frost. In areas that don't freeze, like the South and Pacific West, the seeds can be planted in early spring for summer harvest and early fall for winter harvest.

General Information Concerning Carrots

Carrots require soils that are loose, rich in organic material, and limed. They come in several shapes, each suited for a different type of soil. Long varieties need light soil; medium varieties grow in medium soil; and short varieties grow in heavy soil. Carrot varieties are given at the end of this chapter.

Regardless of the variety, the soil should be free of stones and lumps because they cause the carrots to fork or stop growing. Also, the soil should be rich in potassium, because it gives the carrots a sweet taste. Wood ashes are a good source of potassium. Fertilize the carrots with a fertilizer that has more phosphorous and potassium than nitrogen. Too much nitrogen causes the carrots to be tough and tasteless.

Carrot seeds germinate at a wide range of temperatures varying from 50º to 90º F (10º to 32.2º C). The higher the temperature, the faster the time of germination. Carrots thrive in full sun but tolerate partial shade.

You may grow carrots from seeds or seedlings. Carrot seeds are sold in garden centers, nurseries, and seed catalogs. The latter offer the greatest varieties. They sell packets containing 750 to 1,500 seeds for a price that varies, depending on the variety. Some sell trial-size packets containing fewer seeds for a lower price. You may also buy carrot seeds at a deep discount from some store chains or local discount stores. It is important to choose varieties that are compatible with your soil as explained above.

Carrots may be grown from bought seedlings. Nurseries and garden centers sell 2 or 3 varieties in packs that contain numerous seedlings. Buy varieties that are compatible with your soil. Because carrots grow easily from seeds sown directly in the garden, it doesn't pay to grow seedlings indoors.

Preparing the Soil for Carrots

The Conventional Method: Two weeks before planting, work some organic material such as peat moss or humus at the rate of 4 pounds per 10 square feet into the top 10 inches of the soil. Next, sprinkle 5-10-10 fertilizer at the rate of one cup per 10 square feet and either lime at the rate of one cup per 10 square feet or wood ashes at the rate of 2 cups per 10 square feet. Water thoroughly. Do not use raw manure because it adversely affects the taste of the carrots.

Theresa's Alternative Method: In the area you allocate for carrots, dig 5-inch-wide and 10-inch-deep trenches 12 inches apart for single planting. For wide planting, the maximum trench width should be 16 inches. Prepare potting soil by mixing one part by volume clean topsoil and one part peat moss. Add 2 cups 5-10-10 fertilizer and either 1 cup lime or 2 cups wood ashes to each cubic foot of the potting soil. Fill the trenches with the mix, then water thoroughly.

If you plan to grow carrots in containers, add 1/2 cubic foot perlite or vermiculite and one cup bone meal to each cubic foot of the mix.

Planting Carrots

In cool weather, sow carrot seeds 1/4 inch deep. In warm weather, sow the seeds 1/2 inch deep. This prevents drying of the seeds. Carrot seeds germinate in 6 to 12 days, depending on the weather. To enhance germination, keep the soil moist and warm by covering the area with wet burlap. After one week or so, uncover the burlap to see if the seeds have germinated. When they do, remove the burlap.

In the conventional method, sow the seeds 1/2 inch apart in single rows 12 inches apart or one inch apart in both directions in wide rows. In Theresa's alternative method, sow the seeds 1/2 inch apart in single-row trenches and one inch apart in both directions in wide-row trenches that are filled with potting soil.

You may wish to grow carrot seedlings indoors. Four weeks before the date of last frost, fill 6-inch-deep containers with good potting soil as explained above in Theresa's alternative method. Water thoroughly for a few days. Next, sprinkle the seeds evenly, then cover them with 1/4 inch potting soil. Water lightly once or twice a day until the seeds germinate.

162

Caring for Carrots

The soil should be kept moist at all times. Water lightly twice a day. The most important tasks in caring for carrots are thinning and weeding. When the carrots are about 2 inches high, thin them to 3 inches apart. Meanwhile, cultivate the weeds. Fertilize carrots monthly with 5-10-10 fertilizer at the rate of one cup per 10 feet of single rows or 3 feet of wide rows.

Do not step close to the plants, especially when the soil is wet, in order not to compact the soil. Watch for diseases and insects. In their early stages, they can be managed by pulling the diseased plants and picking the insects.

Harvesting Carrots

Start harvesting the carrots when they reach a reasonable size. This will be about 3 months after planting. Pull the carrots when the soil is wet. If the soil is dry, the carrots will break. Harvest only what you can eat fresh and leave the rest to grow in the ground. Make sure that the carrots are completely covered with soil. The parts that are exposed to the sun become green and taste bitter.

In the North, you may leave the carrots in the ground until early winter, but you have to cover them with mulch before the first frost. In areas where the ground does not freeze, you may keep the carrots in the ground throughout the winter. Carrots store well in the refrigerator for one week or more.

Carrot Diseases

Some of the diseases that infect carrots are bacterial blight, black rot, scab, root rot, leaf spots, and nematodes.

Carrot Insects

The insects that attack carrots include aphids, rust flies, carrot weevils, wireworms, leafhoppers, flea beetles, and nematodes (nematodes are both diseases and insects).

Carrot Varieties

Long: Long varieties include Tendersweet, Sweetness II, Cheyenne, Vita Treat, Annapolis, Sweet Bites, and Caropak.

Medium: Medium varieties include Nantes Coreless, Royal Chantenay, Coreless Amsterdam, Super Mack, and Danvers Half Long.

Short: Short varieties include Baby Finger, Little Finger, Thumbelina, and Healthmaster.

Nutritive Value of Carrots

Carrots are very rich in vitamin A, beta carotene, and potassium. They are also rich in vitamins B, C, D, E, and K and in calcium and phosphorous. Raw carrots contain 35 calories per ounce. Cooked carrots contain 18 calories per ounce.

Chapter 19

Radishes

Radishes germinate and grow faster than any other vegetable. Some varieties can be harvested in as little as 18 days! Radishes come in different shapes and in two colors, red and white.

Time to Plant Radishes

In cool areas like the northern United States and Canada, start sowing radish seeds directly in the ground as soon as the soil can be worked. Make another sowing in late summer or fall, if you have some land available. In the areas that don't freeze, like the South and Pacific West, start sowing spring seeds in late winter for spring harvest and in fall for winter harvest. To extend the harvest season, make successive plantings every 2 weeks.

General Information Concerning Radishes

The maturity of radishes varies from 18 days for the spherical red Saxa variety to 60 days for the long white Japanese Daikon variety. Because of their fast germination, they are often used to mark the rows of other slow-germinating vegetables and herbs such as carrots and parsley. This is accomplished by mixing some radish seeds with the slow-germinating seeds before sowing. In a few days, the radish seeds germinate and there-by mark the rows of both vegetables. This helps in weed cultivation.

The best way to grow radishes is from seeds sown directly in the garden. It is not worth it to grow them from seedlings grown indoors or bought. You may buy seeds from seed catalogs, nurseries, garden centers, or discount stores. The former offer the greatest variety. Seed catalogs sell packets containing 500 seeds. Some sell trial-size packets for some varieties containing 150 seeds for a much lower price. Discount stores offer the least variety but the quality of the seeds is good.

Preparing the Soil for Radishes

The Conventional Method: Two weeks before planting, work some organic material such as peat moss or humus at the rate of 4 pounds per 10 square feet into the top 5 inches of the soil for the spherical red varieties and 8 inches for the long white varieties. Next, sprinkle 5-10-10 fertilizer at the rate of one cup per 10 square feet. Water thoroughly.

Theresa's Alternative Method: In the area you allocate for radishes, dig 5-inch-wide trenches spaced at 12 inches. The depth of the trenches should be 5 inches for the spherical red varieties and 8 inches for the long white varieties. Prepare potting soil consisting of one part by volume clean topsoil and one part peat moss. Add 2 cups 5-10-10 fertilizer to each cubic foot of the potting soil and mix well. Fill the trenches with the mix and water thoroughly.

If you plan to grow radishes in containers, add 1/2 cubic foot perlite or vermiculite and one cup bone meal to each cubic foot of the mix.

Planting Radishes

In the conventional method, sow the seeds one inch apart in rows 12 inches apart. In Theresa's alternative method, sow the seeds one inch apart in the trenches that have been filled with potting soil. In both methods, cover the seeds with 1/2 inch soil. Firm the soil over the seeds with the back of a rake, then water thoroughly.

If you are sowing radish seeds mixed with other slow-germinating seeds, follow the planting directions of the other seeds.

Caring for Radishes

Keep the area around the radishes free of weeds. When the seedlings reach 2 inches high, thin them to 2 inches apart by pulling every second one. Water daily. Lack of water causes the radishes to be bitter and pungent. Fertilize the radishes every month with 5-10-10 fertilizer at the rate of one cup per 10 feet of row or trench. Watch for diseases and insects.

Harvesting Radishes

Harvest the radishes when they reach an edible size. Pull all the radishes before the leaves turn yellow. Remove the green tops and store the radishes in the refrigerator. They store for more than a week.

Radish Diseases

Radish diseases include black rot, downy mildew, powdery mildew, leaf spots, scab, club root, white rust, and radish mosaic.

Radish Insects

Radish insects include cabbage maggots, wireworms, leaf miners, aphids, flea beetles, cabbage loopers, and imported cabbageworms.

Radish Varieties

Radish varieties are either spherical or long. The following are some of both varieties and the days to maturity.

Spherical: Spherical varieties include Saxa (18), German Giant (29), Champion (27), Easter Egg (28), Cherry Belle (22), Sparkler (25), Big Ben (29), Fancy Red (26), Crimson Giant (30), and Snow Belle (28).

Long: Long varieties include Long White Icicle (27), Japanese Daikon (60), and French Breakfast (25).

Nutritive Value of Radishes

Radishes contain vitamin C and calcium, phosphorous, and potassium. Each ounce contains 7.9 calories.

Part 4

Tender Vegetables

Chapters in This Part

Chapter 20

Tomatoes

T omatoes are the king of the vegetable garden. If we were to grow only one vegetable plant, it would be a tomato. This is because home-grown tomatoes are far superior in taste, freshness, and nutritive value to those that are sold in the market. Most of the tomatoes sold in the stores are picked green, then sprayed with a gas to give them red color. The reason is that commercial tomatoes must be hard and tough to withstand shipping and staying on the shelves for days. If tomatoes are picked ripe and then shipped, they will rot before reaching the stores. Some supermarkets sell Holland, hothouse, and vine-ripe tomatoes that have some taste in them, but their price is steep, up to $4 a pound. A big-producer variety such as Beefsteak, Beefmaster, or Sweet 100 can yield 10 or more pounds per plant. Imagine, one plant produces up to $40 worth of tomatoes!

A big-producer variety such as Beefmaster can yield 10 or more pounds per plant.

Time to Plant Tomatoes

In cool areas like the northern United States and Canada, tomatoes should be planted outdoors after the danger of frost is gone and the minimum night temperature exceeds 45º F (7.2º C). In areas that don't freeze, like the South and Pacific West, start planting tomatoes outdoors in late winter and early spring, depending on the climate.

General Information Concerning Tomatoes

Tomato plants have several virtues that make them appealing to home gardeners: (1) they are easy to grow, (2) they can withstand an overnight cold spell as low as 40º F (4.4º C), (3) they take transplanting well, and (4) their roots are extensive and deep, which enables them to absorb nutrients and water from deep below.

One peculiar characteristic of tomato plants is that they hate smoking! If someone smokes near them, they can be afflicted with tobacco mosaic, a disease that reduces productivity. Some tomato strains are bred to resist tobacco mosaic, but it is advisable to refrain from smoking in the presence of tomato plants.

Tomatoes come in different sizes, from the huge Beefmaster to the tiny Sweet 100. Some are good for slicing while others are good for juicing. All are good for fresh eating.

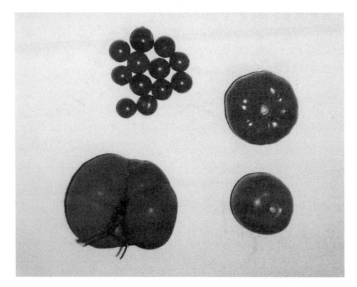

Tomatoes come in different sizes from the huge Beefmaster to the tiny Sweet 100.

Tomato plants are classified as determinate or indeterminate. Determinate plants are bushy and grow to 3 feet. They produce all their fruit at one time, then die. The advantage of determinate plants is that they mature faster than indeterminate plants, which is good in areas that have a short season like the extreme northern parts of the United States and Canada. Their disadvantage is that they don't produce as much as indeterminate varieties.

Indeterminate plants grow big and need support. They keep growing and producing continuously until frost kills them. They produce heavily, especially if the weather cooperates. Most tomato varieties are indeterminate.

Virtually all tomato seeds and seedlings sold today are bred to resist diseases. Seed packets and seedlings have abbreviations to indicate the diseases the seeds resist. The most common abbreviations and their meaning are:

"**V**" indicates resistant to Verticillium Wilt.
"**F**" indicates resistant to Fusarium Wilt, Race I.
"**FF**" indicates resistant to Fusarium Wilt, Races I and II.
"**N**" indicates resistant to Nematodes.
"**T**" indicates resistant to Tobacco Mosaic.

Generally, tomato seeds and seedlings are bred to resist more than one disease. For example, a seed packet or seedling pack labeled VFN indicates that the seeds resist 3 of the diseases indicated above. Buy seeds and seedlings that resist as many diseases as possible.

You may grow tomatoes from seeds sown directly in the garden, from seedlings grown indoors, or bought. Seeds may be bought from nurseries, garden centers, discount stores, or seed catalogs. Seed catalogs offer many varieties. Some seed catalogs offer seed varieties they claim can withstand frost, but our experience with these seeds is not satisfactory. Discount stores offer limited varieties but the quality is good.

As a general rule, the bigger the variety the longer it takes to mature. Big varieties take up to 80 days from transplanting to the first fruit. Medium and small varieties take 65 to 70 days to maturity.

To grow seedlings indoors, you should use the proper heating and lighting equipment. Tomato seeds germinate best when the day temperature is 80° F (26.7° C) and the night temperature is 60° F (15.6° C). If you live in an environment where the indoor temperature is about 70° F (21.1° C) day and night, the seedlings will grow leggy, meaning long weak stems and small leaves. An alternative is to place the seedlings on the sill of a bay or bow window facing south during the day and move them to a cool place, such as an unheated basement, during the night.

Growing tomatoes from seedlings you buy is a good choice. Local nurs-

Tip

Use the following technique to advance the time of harvest by 3 weeks. Buy tomato seedlings as soon as they are offered for sale, usually 3 to 4 weeks before they can be transplanted outdoors. Immediately transplant them into bigger pots or containers, then fertilize them with 5-10-5 or 5-10-10 fertilizer at the rate of one tablespoon per seedling. When the weather is sunny and warm, take them outdoors. At night or when the weather is cold, move them indoors. By the time the weather permits their transplant in the garden, the seedlings should have grown much bigger. Transplant the seedlings with as much soil around the roots as possible.

eries and garden centers offer several varieties. They sell them in packs each containing 4 to 6 seedlings. When buying seedlings, choose short ones with thick erect stems and big green leaves. Also, look at the bottom of the cells. If the roots are coming out through the drain holes, don't buy them.

Preparing the Soil for Tomatoes

The Conventional Method: Two weeks before sowing the seeds or transplanting, work organic material such as peat moss, humus, or composted manure into the top 8 inches of the soil at the rate of 4 pounds per 10 square feet. Double this rate if the soil is hard or if the plot was not used to grow vegetables before. Additionally, sprinkle 5-10-10 fertilizer at the rate of one cup per 10 square feet. Pick and kill any insects you may find while working the soil. Water thoroughly. If rain is forecast, Mother Nature will water your garden for free.

Theresa's Alternative Method: In the area you allocate for tomatoes, dig holes 15 inches across and 10 inches deep, spaced 3 feet apart. Prepare potting soil by mixing one part by volume clean topsoil, one part peat moss, and one part composted manure. Add 5-10-10 fertilizer at the rate of 2 cups per cubic foot of the potting soil. Mix well, then fill the holes. Water thoroughly.

If you plan to grow tomatoes in containers, replace the composted manure with one part perlite or vermiculite and add one cup bone meal to each cubic foot of the mix.

Planting Tomatoes

You may sow tomato seeds directly in the garden when the minimum ambient temperature exceeds 60º F (15.6º C). It is practical to sow tomato seeds directly in the garden only in warm areas.

In the conventional method, sow the seeds every 12 inches and cover with 1/2 inch soil. When the seedlings grow to 4 inches high, thin them to 3 feet apart. If you grow from seedlings, transplant them 3 feet apart. One mistake beginners make is to plant tomatoes close to each other. After a few weeks, the plants grow big and touch each other, which retards their growth and makes walking among them almost impossible.

In Theresa's alternative method, sow 2 seeds in each hole filled with potting soil. When the seedlings grow to 3 inches high, keep the stronger seedling and pinch or transplant the other one. If you grow from seedlings, plant one seedling in each hole.

In both methods, cut off the bottom leaves of each seedling, then bury the stem in the soil as deeply as possible. The part of the stem buried in the soil will grow roots, which enhances the growth of the plant. Firm the soil around the stems with the palm of your hand (always wear gloves). Water thoroughly.

If you want to grow tomatoes from seedlings grown indoors, start 6 to 8 weeks before the last frost. Fill a container, pot, or tray with potting soil as described above in Theresa's alternative method. Sow the seeds 1/2 inch deep and 2 inches apart. Water daily. However, it has been our experience that growing tomato seedlings indoors is time consuming and the plants produced are inferior to those we buy from local nurseries.

Caring for Tomatoes

The main effort in caring for tomato plants is to prevent the weeds from taking over. They rob the plants of the nutrients they need to grow and give a good harvest. Use black plastic sheet as mulch. Place a cage around each seedling to provide support when the seedlings grow.

For bigger yield, tomato plants should be pruned continuously. Leave only one or two big stems and cut the suckers as soon as they appear. The suckers are the beginnings of new stems. They grow from a stem above a leaf. If left to grow, the plants grow more leaves and less fruit.

Tomatoes need a lot of water and fertilizers. They should be watered daily, unless it rains. If it rains 1/2 inch or more, skip watering for 2 days. Tomatoes should be fed by 5-10-10 fertilizer at the rate of 1/2 cup per plant per month.

When the weather becomes very hot and dry, tomatoes may be afflicted with sunscald. It starts with large, light yellowish spots that appear on the portion of unripe tomatoes facing the sun. As the tomatoes ripen, the spot turns whitish. To prevent sunscald, cover the fruits facing the sun during hot dry spells. Discard the tomatoes that are afflicted with sunscald.

When the weather becomes very hot and dry, tomatoes may be afflicted with sunscald.

Harvesting Tomatoes

Harvesting tomatoes is the biggest fun. As soon as a tomato ripens and becomes red, pick and enjoy eating it. Tomatoes ripen from the inside out. Therefore, you may pick them as soon as they start to color and keep them in a cool spot away from sunlight. They will ripen in a few days. The taste will be like those that ripen on the vine. We usually pick them before they ripen fully when we notice that animals start eating them. Rats, squirrels, and woodchucks sometimes eat tomatoes, but only when they are fully ripe!

Harvesting tomatoes is the biggest fun. Wasfi proudly holds 2 huge Beefmaster tomatoes.

If you go on a vacation, collect the big green tomatoes and store them side by side in a cool dark place (the cellar, for example). By the time you come back, many of them will be ready for eating.

At the end of the season, when frost is forecast, pick all the tomatoes from the vines and store them as explained above. Alternatively, dig up the plants with some soil around their roots. Place each plant in a container and move them indoors. You will eat fresh tomatoes until Christmas!

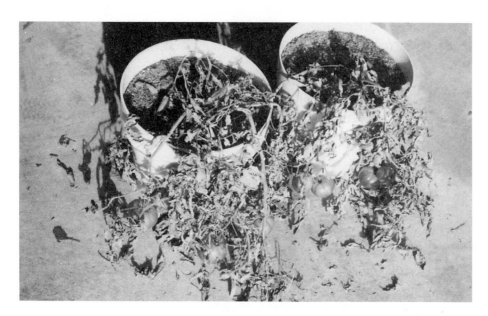

You will eat fresh tomatoes until Christmas, if at the end of the season you dig up the plants with some soil around the roots and place each plant in a container.

Tomato Diseases

Tomato diseases include leaf spots, bacterial wilt, bacterial spot, downy mildew, powdery mildew, tobacco mosaic, anthracnose, scab, verticillium wilt, fusarium wilt, sunscald, early and late blight, and nematodes.

Tomato Insects

Tomato insects include cutworms, tomato hornworms, aphids, slugs, fiea beetles, Colorado potato beetles, corn earworms, cabbage loopers, stinkbugs, and whiteflies.

Tomato Varieties

Tomatoes are grouped according to their size into big, medium, and small.

Big: Big varieties weigh one or more pounds per fruit. They include Beefmaster, Beefsteak, and Super Beefsteak.

Medium: Medium varieties weigh 1/2 to one pound apiece. They include Early Girl, Celebrity, Big Boy, Better Boy, Lemon Boy (yellow), Rutgers, Miracle Sweet, and Big Beef.

Small: Small varieties weigh about an ounce each. They include Sweet 100, Super Sweet 100, Red Cherry, Supersonic, and Patio.

Nutritive Value of Tomatoes

Tomatoes are rich in vitamins A, B, and C and in potassium, phosphorous, calcium, and iron. Raw tomatoes contain only 5.5 calories per ounce. This means that a 1/2-pound tomato contains only 44 calories.

Chapter 21

Summer Squashes

Summer squashes are either green (zucchini) or yellow (straightneck and crookneck). We plant both varieties, but prefer the zucchini because it is tenderer and tastier. The small ones are so tender that some people eat them raw.

Summer squashes may be grilled and fried and made into soups, casseroles, stews, and cakes. They produce so heavily that you don't know what to do with the surplus. To help you in this regard, we include at the end of this chapter a few recipes that are easy to prepare.

Time to Plant Summer Squashes

In cool areas like the northern United States and Canada, the time to plant summer squashes is after the danger of frost is gone. This would be mid to late spring. In the areas that don't freeze, like the South and Pacific West, summer squashes can be planted in early to mid spring.

General Information Concerning
Summer Squashes

Summer squashes are popular with gardeners, because they are prolific producers and easy to grow. A few plants provide a family with all it can eat. If you want your summer squash plants to produce heavily, give them plenty of water and fertilize them frequently.

Summer squashes may be grown from seeds sown directly in the garden, seedlings grown indoors, or seedlings bought. Seeds are sold in nurseries, garden centers, seed catalogs, and discount stores. Seed catalogs offer the greatest variety. Unless you want to grow a specific variety, buy seeds at a discount store for as little as 10 cents for a packet containing 7 seeds.

You may buy summer squash seedlings from a nearby nursery or garden center. They sell packs containing 4 to 6 cells with each cell containing 3 to 4 seedlings. The quality is usually good. Buy them when you are ready to transplant them (keeping them in small cells for a long time retards the growth of the plants). Buy healthy plants with shiny green leaves.

Preparing the Soil for Summer Squashes

The Conventional Method: Two weeks before planting, work organic matter such as peat moss, humus, or dehydrated manure into the top 10 inches of the soil at the rate of 4 pounds per 10 square feet. Sprinkle 10-10-10 fertilizer at the rate of one cup per 10 square feet. Water thoroughly.

Theresa's Alternative Method: In the area you allocate for summer squashes, dig 10-inch-deep and 15-inch-across holes 4 feet apart. Fill the holes with potting soil consisting of one part by volume clean topsoil, one part peat moss, and one part dehydrated manure. Add 2 cups 10-10-10 fertilizer to each cubic foot of potting soil. Mix well. Fill the holes with the mix, then water thoroughly.

If you want to grow summer squashes in containers, replace the dehydrated manure with one part perlite or vermiculite and add one cup bone meal to each cubic foot of the mix.

Planting Summer Squashes

To grow summer squashes from seeds sown directly in the ground, wait until the day high temperature exceeds 75º F (23.9º C). The seeds should be sown one inch deep in hills each containing 3 or 4 seeds. The seed germination rate for summer squashes is very high.

To grow summer squash seedlings indoors, start 2 weeks before the danger of frost has passed. Sow 3 or 4 seeds in 3-inch individual pots filled with good potting soil as explained above in Theresa's alternative method. This gives the roots room to grow and does not disturb the roots during transplanting in the garden. If you want healthy seedlings, buy heating and lighting equipment. If not, place the pots in a sunny spot such as a window sill facing south during the day and a cool place such as an unheated basement during the night.

To grow summer squashes from seedlings grown indoors or bought, empty the content of each cell or pot every 4 feet. Do not separate the individual seedlings because this kills them. Transplant the seedlings on a cloudy day or after sunset to prevent their dehydration. Don't transplant if the following day is forecast to be seasonally hot.

In the conventional method, plant summer squashes every 4 feet in rows 4 feet apart. In Theresa's alternative method, sow one hill or empty the content of one cell or pot in each hole filled with potting soil. In both methods, firm the soil around the seedlings, then water thoroughly.

Caring for Summer Squashes

Summer squashes are big feeders. They should be watered daily and fertilized with 10-10-10 fertilizer once a month at the rate of 1/2 cup per hill. Don't drop fertilizers over the leaves or the stem because this burns them. A good time to fertilize the plants is before rainfall.

Weeds are less of a problem for grown summer squashes because the latter's big leaves obstruct the growth of the weeds. Watch for diseases and insects. If you see a worm inside a squash, throw it away. If the worms persist, you may have to use a pesticide. Take a sample to a big nursery and the staff will identify the problem and give you an insecticide. It has been our experience that if you keep the garden clean, worms do not appear.

Harvesting Summer Squashes

Summer squashes mature in about 6 weeks after transplanting. Each plant produces both male and female flowers. The male flowers bloom first, and the female flowers bloom about 10 days later. We explained earlier how to distinguish between male and female squash flowers.

Harvest the squashes when they are 6 to 8 inches long, because they taste best when small. Cut them with a knife or twist them. Because summer squashes grow fast, they should be picked daily. If not, they will grow huge in a matter of days. Look carefully under the leaves. So often, we find gigantic squashes that we failed to see because they were hidden under the big leaves. If summer squashes grow too big, they form seeds, and the plants stop producing and die.

Summer squashes are so prolific that you won't know what to do with them. They can be stored in the refrigerator for a week or two without losing too much flavor. The best way to dispose of the surplus is to give them to neighbors, friends, and relatives, or to a soup kitchen, if there is one nearby.

Summer Squash Diseases

The diseases that attack summer squashes include bacterial wilt, bacterial spot, downy mildew, powdery mildew, leaf blight, mosaic virus, anthracnose, fusarium wilt, root rot, and scab.

Summer Squash Insects

Summer squash insects include nematodes, aphids, squash vine borers, corn earworms, leafhoppers, whiteflies, and squash bugs.

Summer Squash Varieties

Green: Green varieties include Black Zucchini, Jackpot, Spacemiser, Black Magic, and Garden Spineless.

Yellow: Yellow varieties include Gold Rush, Golden Summer Crookneck, Crescent, Butterstick, and Prolific Straightneck.

Nutritive Value of Summer Squashes

Summer squashes contain potassium, calcium, and vitamins A and C. Cooked squash contains 5.5 calories per ounce.

Recipes for Summer Squashes

1. Grilled Zucchini: Grilled zucchini is nutritious, tasty, and light. We learned this simple recipe from the Crown Plaza Hotel in White Plains, New York. They include grilled zucchini as a side vegetable with egg plates for breakfast. The zucchini was so delicious that we asked the waitress for the recipe. She answered that it is very simple: the zucchini is sliced, sprinkled with spices, then grilled. Ever since, throughout the season, we grill zucchini and use it as a side vegetable for any meal.

2. Zucchini Soup: We use this recipe for the first zucchini we harvest, because it is extremely tender and tasty. We add sliced small zucchini to 2 cups of chicken or beef broth, boil it for 5 to 7 minutes, and then serve hot. The zucchini adds nutrients to the broth and the taste is fantastic.

3. Baked Zucchini Casserole: This is a recipe in which we use zucchini, pepper, onions, and tomato juice, all fresh from the garden. This meal costs about 70 cents per serving.

Ingredients for 8 Servings

2 pounds ground beef
2 medium onions, chopped
3 cups of freshly squeezed tomato juice
Salt and pepper to taste
3 pounds zucchini
1 bell pepper or 2 frying peppers (for seasoning)

Cooking Directions

Place the ground beef, chopped onions, tomato juice, salt, and pepper in a pan. No butter or oil is needed because the ground beef contains fat. Bring to a boil while stirring continuously. Cook over medium heat until the ground beef becomes brown (about 15 minutes).

Cut the zucchini into 3/8-inch-thick 3-inch-long slices. Cut the peppers into thin slices. Lay the zucchini and pepper slices in a casserole. Spread the ground beef mix on top of the zucchini and pepper and cover completely. Cover the casserole with aluminum foil. This speeds up cooking and keeps the meal moist.

Place the casserole in a 350° F (176.7° C) preheated oven for about 30 minutes. Remove the aluminum foil and raise the oven temperature to 450° F (232.2° C). Leave the casserole for 5 minutes until the top takes on a brown color. Remove from the oven and serve. Refrigerate the leftovers.

Chapter 22

Sweet Corn

Sweet corn is bred to be sweeter than ordinary corn. It requires full sun and soil rich in nitrogen. One characteristic of sweet corn is that its sugar starts to be converted into starch after it is harvested. As a result, it loses its sweetness. Fortunately, new varieties are being developed to lengthen the time the corn stays sweet after harvest.

Time to Plant Sweet Corn

In cool areas like the northern United States and Canada, sweet corn should be planted after the danger of frost is gone and the maximum day temperature exceeds 70° F (21.1° C). In the areas that don't freeze, like the South and Pacific West, sweet corn can be planted in mid to late winter.

General Information Concerning Sweet Corn

Most sweet corn varieties are yellow, but some are white while others are mixed white and yellow. All sweet corn varieties are hybrid. Sweet corn is divided into 3 groups. These groups and their abbreviations are:

Sugary Enhanced Hybrid (**SE** or **se**).
Super-Sweet Hybrid (**SH2** or **sh2**).
High Sugar Hybrid (**SU** or **su**).

For good pollination, corn should be planted in 4 or more rows, spaced 2 feet apart. The seeds must be from the same group in all rows to prevent cross-pollination, which results in starchy rather than sweet corn. If you plan to use seeds from more than one group, keep the plants at least 300 feet apart. If your neighbor is growing corn close to yours, you should coordinate with her the seed group each of you uses in order to prevent cross-pollination between your corn and hers.

Sweet corn may be grown from seeds sown directly in the ground, seedlings grown indoors, or seedlings you buy. Seeds may be bought from seed catalogs, nurseries, garden centers, and discount stores. The former offer the biggest varieties. The price varies for packets containing 70 to 250 seeds (the better the variety, the higher the price). It is recommended that you review one or more seed catalogs in order to have a good idea about corn varieties and their prices before buying.

Seedlings may be bought from nurseries or garden centers. When you buy sweet corn seedlings, don't buy seedlings that are very close to each other, in order not to disturb the roots during transplanting. Additionally, the seedlings you buy should be strong and healthy.

Preparing the Soil for Sweet Corn

The Conventional Method: Two weeks before planting, work organic material such as peat moss, humus, or composted manure at the rate of 4 pounds per 10 square feet into the top 8 inches of the soil. Next, sprinkle 10-10-10 fertilizer at the rate of one cup per 10 square feet. Water thoroughly.

Theresa's Alternative Method: In the area you allocate for sweet corn, dig 4 parallel trenches spaced 2 feet apart. The trenches should be 6 inches wide and 6 inches deep. Fill the trenches with potting soil consisting of one part by volume clean topsoil, one part peat moss, and one part composted manure. Add one cup 10-10-10 fertilizer to each cubic foot of the potting soil. Mix well, then fill the trenches with the mix. Water thoroughly.

Planting Sweet Corn

In the conventional method, to grow sweet corn from seeds sown directly in the garden, sow the seeds 6 inches apart and 3/4 inch deep. Plant in 4 or more rows spaced 2 feet apart. When the seedlings become 6 inches high, thin them to 12 inches apart. To grow corn from seedlings grown indoors or bought, transplant one seedling every 12 inches. In Theresa's alternative method, plant sweet corn in the trenches that are filled with potting soil following the same procedure.

If you want to grow seedlings indoors, start 4 weeks before the last frost. Using the proper heating and lighting equipment is important for healthy seedlings. Corn roots are easily disturbed during transplanting. Therefore, use 3-inch pots and sow 2 seeds in each pot. When the seedlings are about 2 inches high, cut the weaker and leave the stronger. Empty the contents of each pot in one spot. This way, the roots will not be disturbed during transplanting.

Caring for Sweet Corn

Sweet corn should be watered daily and fertilized monthly with 10-10-10 fertilizer at the rate of one cup per 10 feet of row. Keep the plants 12 inches apart. If a seedling dies, replace it with a seedling from those that have been thinned or sow 2 seeds in its place. When they germinate, keep the stronger seedling and cut the other.

Weeds should be cultivated regularly. Use black plastic mulch to prevent the weeds from growing, to keep the soil warm, and to save water. Watch for diseases and insects, especially worms. When the silk develops, uncover the upper portion of some ears regularly to see if there are any worms. If so, take a sample to a big nursery to identify the worm and recommend a pesticide. Follow the manufacturer's instructions.

Harvesting Sweet Corn

Sweet corn is harvested when the kernel is fully developed. Cut what you intend to cook, because corn loses its sweetness quickly. Ears grown from good-quality seeds can stay sweet for a couple of days.

Sweet Corn Diseases

Sweet corn diseases include bacterial wilt, bacterial rot, ear rot, black rot, bacterial spots, leaf blight, corn smut, fusarium rot, and corn mosaic virus.

Sweet Corn Insects

Some of the insects that attack sweet corn are European corn borers, corn earworms, flea beetles, corn rootworms, Japanese beetles, leaf miners, striped cucumber beetles, root webworms, seed-corn maggots, and wireworms.

Sweet Corn Varieties

SE Group: SE group includes Kandy Korn, Cotton Candy (white), Double Delicious, Buttergold, Frosty, Peaches and Cream, Incredible, Bodacious, Kandy King, and Trinity.

SH2 Group: SH2 group includes Early Xrta-Sweet, Illini Xtra-Sweet, Northern Xtra Sweet, Mini Sweet, Supersweet Jubilee, Sweet Heart, How Sweet It Is (white), Indian Summer, Fortune, Odyssey, and Majesty.

SU Group: SU group includes NK-199, Bi-Licious, Polar Vee, Silver Queen (white), Early Sunglow, and Iochief.

Nutritive Value of Sweet Corn

Sweet corn is rich in potassium and vitamin E. It also contains vitamins B and C and phosphorous.

Chapter 23

Beans

Beans are grouped into bush, pole, shell, and lima. The bush beans are popular with home gardeners because they are compact and don't need support. Furthermore, they can be grown in containers. Pole beans produce more than bush but need support.

Time to Plant Beans

In cool areas like the northern United States and Canada, beans should be planted after the danger of frost is gone and the high day temperature exceeds 70º F (21.1º C). In the areas that don't freeze, like the South and Pacific West, plant beans in late winter to early spring for early summer harvest and in the fall for a winter crop. For a longer harvest season, make successive plantings of bush beans every 2 weeks.

General Information Concerning Beans

Beans are legumes, which means that their roots have bacteria that absorb nitrogen from the air and fix it in the soil and on the plant's roots. As a result, beans should be fertilized with a fertilizer that contains less nitrogen than phosphorous or potassium.

Beans may be grown from seeds sown directly in the garden or in containers. It is not recommended that you grow beans from seedlings grown indoors or bought, because it is not worth it.

You may buy bean seeds from seed catalogs, nurseries, garden centers, or discount stores. Seed catalogs exhibit many varieties. They sell them in 2-ounce, 1/2-pound, and one-pound packets. Nurseries and garden centers sell bean packets at the list price or slightly less. Deeply discounted seed packets contain a fraction of an ounce. Since beans are easy to grow from seeds sown directly in the ground, it doesn't pay to grow them from seedlings.

Bush beans come in different colors: green, yellow (wax), and purple. The latter turn green when cooked. Pole beans come in green and yellow (wax). All bush bean varieties grow well in containers.

Coating bean seeds with an inoculant, which is a bacterium that fixes nitrogen it absorbs from the air in the soil, improves the yield. Some seed catalogs sell a one-ounce packet of inoculant for $1. It is not worth it to buy an inoculant unless you plant a big area.

Preparing the Soil for Beans

The Conventional Method: One week before sowing the seeds, work some organic material such as peat moss or humus at the rate of 2 pounds per 10 square feet into the top 5 inches of the soil. Next, sprinkle

5-10-10 fertilizer at the rate of one cup per 20 square feet. Water thoroughly.

Theresa's Alternative Method: In the area you designate for growing beans, dig trenches 5 inches deep and 5 inches wide spaced 12 inches apart for single-row planting. For wide-row planting dig trenches 5 inches deep and up to 16 inches wide. Fill the trenches with potting soil consisting of one part by volume clean topsoil and one part peat moss. Add one cup 5-10-10 fertilizer to each cubic foot of potting soil and mix well. Fill the trenches with the mix, then water thoroughly. If you plan to grow beans in containers, add 1/2 cubic foot perlite or vermiculite and one cup bone meal to each cubic foot of the mix.

Planting Beans

Because beans are easy to grow from seeds sown directly in the garden, this is the method we recommend. All bean seeds should be sown one inch deep. In the conventional method, plant beans in single rows 12 inches apart or up to 16-inch-wide rows. Sow the seeds 2 inches apart for bush beans and 4 inches apart for all other beans (pole, shell, and dried). Firm the soil over the beans and water thoroughly. In Theresa's alternative method, sow bean seeds in the trenches that are filled with potting soil following the procedure explained above.

To grow bush beans in containers, fill them with potting soil as explained above in Theresa's alternative method. Sow the seeds one inch deep and 2 inches apart in both directions. Firm the soil over the seeds, then water thoroughly.

Caring for Beans

Beans should be watered daily and fed monthly with 5-10-10 fertilizer at the rate of one cup per 10 feet of single rows and 4 feet of wide rows. Watch for diseases and insects. If you see Japanese beetles, erect 1 or 2 beetle traps in the place recommended by the manufacturer. Weeds are less of a problem for bush beans planted as described above. However, the weeds should be cultivated while small. Use black plastic sheets between the rows or trenches as mulch.

Harvesting Beans

Bush: Most bush bean varieties mature in 2 months. All pods mature at the same time. Harvest them when the pods are full and tender. After picking all pods, turn the plants under to enrich the soil and plant another crop in their place if the weather permits.

Pole: Pole beans keep producing until frost. They should be harvested regularly when the pods are full and crisp. When the night temperature reaches 50º F (10º C), pick all pods. Frost kills beans and makes them inedible.

Shell: Shell beans should be harvested when pods are fully developed and their color starts to change. Pick all pods when the night temperature reaches 50º F.

Lima: Harvest lima beans when pods are fully developed.

Bean Diseases

Bean diseases include mosaic virus, downy mildew, powdery mildew, bacterial blight, bacterial wilt, bacterial spots, leaf spots, white mold, anthracnose, and nematodes.

Bean Insects

Bean insects include Mexican bean beetles, leaf beetles, leafhoppers, aphids, leaf miners, seed-corn maggots, stinkbugs, cutworms, wireworms, whiteflies, and corn earworms.

Bean Varieties

Bush: Bush bean varieties include Topcrop (disease resistant), Blue Lake 274 (disease resistant), Bush Kentucky Wonder, Florence, Derby (disease resistant), Tenderette, Purple Queen (purple, disease resistant), Royal Burgundy (purple, resists Mexican bean beetles), Golden Wax (yellow),

Cherokee (yellow), E-Z Gold (yellow, disease resistant), Goldkist (yellow, disease resistant), Masai, Purple Teepee, Benchmark, and Gold Rush (yellow).

Pole: Pole bean varieties include Kentucky Blue, Kentucky Wonder, Blue Lake, Purple Pod (purple), Romano, and Kentucky Wonder Wax (yellow).

Shell: Shell bean varieties include California Blackeye Cowpea, Jacob's Cattle, Dwarf Horticultural, Pinto, and Dark Red Kidney.

Lima: Lima bean varieties include Fordhook 242, Henderson, Jackson Wonder, Eastland, Speckled Calico, and King of the Garden.

Nutritive Value of Beans

All beans are rich in vitamins A and B and potassium. They also contain calcium, phosphorous, iron, and vitamin C. There are 10.2 calories in each ounce.

Part 5
Very-Tender Vegetables

Chapters in This Part

Chapter 24

Peppers

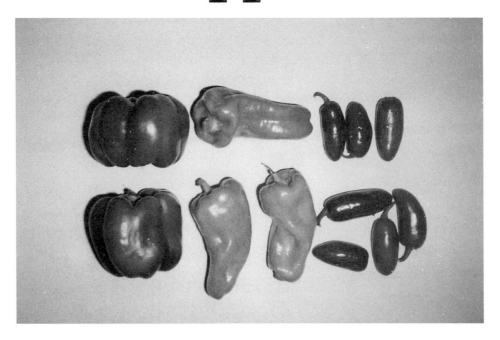

Peppers are divided into sweet and hot. Hot peppers are an important ingredient in Mexican and Indian foods. Both sweet and hot peppers can be eaten raw, in salads, or pickled. They can also be used to flavor stews, tomato sauces, and soups, and as pizza topping and for stuffing. A recipe for stuffed peppers is presented at the end of this chapter.

Time to Plant Peppers

Plant peppers when the high day temperature exceeds 80° F (26.7° C). In the northern United States and Canada, that would be 2 weeks after the date of last frost. In the South and Pacific West, that would be in late winter or early spring.

General Information Concerning Peppers

The optimum temperature for pepper seed germination is 80° to 90° F (26.7° to 32.2° C). At lower temperatures, the seeds take longer to germinate. If the ambient temperature falls below 50° F (10° C) or rises above 90° F (32.2° C) for several consecutive days, some of the blossoms and small peppers fall off. To give a good yield, peppers need 4 to 5 months of warm weather.

It is important to note that pepper plants require a considerable amount of magnesium. Dissolve 1/2 tablespoon of Epsom salt (magnesium sulfate) in a quart (about one liter) of water and pour it over each plant. Please note that magnesium can be absorbed by pepper plants only if the pH value of the soil is between 6.0 and 6.5. If your soil is too acidic, meaning pH is less than 6.0, add lime to the soil at the rate of one tablespoon per plant. Do not plant sweet and hot peppers close to each other, because they will cross-pollinate.

You may grow peppers from seeds sown directly in the ground, seedlings you grow indoors, or seedlings you buy. Seeds can be bought from seed catalogs, garden centers, nurseries, or discount stores. Seed catalogs offer the greatest variety. Some offer trial-size packets of some varieties at a fraction of the price of standard packets.

Any one-inch-deep container can be used to grow pepper seedlings.

Because peppers need several months of warm weather to grow, sowing seeds directly in the garden is not suited for the northern United States and Canada. To gain time, buy seedlings as early as possible from nurseries that keep them in greenhouses. Transplant them into bigger pots and keep them indoors for a few days. Gradually, bring them outdoors when it is sunny and the ambient temperature exceeds 70º F (21.1º C). This allows the roots to expand and the plants to grow. As stated earlier, transplant them in the garden when the high day temperature exceeds 80º F (26.7º C).

Preparing the Soil for Peppers

The Conventional Method: Two weeks before transplanting, work organic material such as peat moss, humus, or composted manure into the top 6 inches of the soil at the rate of 3 pounds per 10 square feet. Additionally, sprinkle 5-10-10 fertilizer at the rate of one cup per 10 square feet. Water thoroughly.

Theresa's Alternative Method: In the area you allocate for peppers, dig holes 10 inches wide and 6 inches deep spaced at 1 1/2 feet. Prepare potting soil consisting of one part by volume clean topsoil, one part peat moss, and one part composted manure. Add 2 cups 5-10-10 fertilizer to each cubic foot of the potting soil and mix well. Fill the holes with the mix and water thoroughly.

If you plan to grow peppers in containers, replace the composted manure with one part perlite or vermiculite and add one cup bone meal to each cubic foot of the mix.

Planting Peppers

To grow peppers from seeds sown directly in the garden, in the conventional method sow the seeds every 6 inches in rows spaced at 1 1/2 feet. When the seedlings grow to 4 inches high, thin them to 1 1/2 feet apart. In Theresa's alternative method, sow 2 seeds in each hole. When the seedlings grow to 4 inches high, keep the stronger seedling and transplant or cut the weaker one. In both methods, the seeds should be sown 1/2 inch deep.

To grow pepper seedlings indoors, start 4 weeks before the last frost. Use proper heating and lighting equipment; otherwise, the seedlings will grow weak and leggy. The effort and cost of starting indoors are justified if you plan to grow many plants or if you want to grow specific varieties that are not sold as seedlings in local nurseries.

Caring for Peppers

It is recommended that you cover the area around pepper plants with black plastic sheets. Water the peppers daily and soak them (1/2 inch water) once a week. If heavy rain is forecast, Mother Nature will water your plants for free. Peppers should be fertilized every month at the rate of 1/4 cup 5-10-10 fertilizer per plant. Watch for diseases and insects.

It is recommended that you cover the area around pepper plants with black plastic sheets.

Harvesting Peppers

Sweet peppers may be harvested when they reach a reasonable size. Pick the peppers continuously to make the plants produce more. Do not pull the peppers because you may break the vines. Rather, cut the peppers with a knife or a pair of scissors. Wear protective gloves when picking hot peppers. Don't get hot peppers close to your eyes. Eat or cook peppers shortly after they are picked to preserve their flavor and vitamin content. Store what you cannot eat in the refrigerator. Peppers store well for a few days. At the end of the season, if frost is forecast, either cover the plants or pick all the peppers regardless of their size and store them in the refrigerator.

Pepper Diseases

The most common pepper diseases include cucumber mosaic virus, tobacco mosaic virus, potato virus, bacterial spot, bacterial wilt, blight, anthracnose, downy mildew, nematodes, sunscald, fusarium wilt, verticillium wilt, and blossom rot blight.

Pepper Insects

Several insects attack sweet peppers. (Not many insects dare to attack hot peppers!) They include pepper maggots, pepper weevils, Colorado potato beetles, cutworms, corn earworms, tomato hornworms, leaf miners, leafhoppers, European corn borers, and aphids. Aphids are serious in that they transmit diseases, particularly cucumber mosaic virus, to pepper plants.

Pepper Varieties

Sweet: Sweet pepper varieties include Whopper Improved, Bell Boy, King of the North, Golden Summer (disease resistant), Lilac, Crispy Bell, Red Beauty, Sweet Banana, Cubanelle, Big Bertha, California Wonder, Big Red, Candy Bar, Golden Summer, and Big Belle.

Hot: Hot pepper varieties include Ancho, Cayenne, Jalapeno, Garden Salsa, Super Chili, Anaheim TMR, Habanero (very hot), Tabasco, Tears of Fire, Thai Dragon, and Giant Thai Hot.

Nutritive Value of Peppers

Sweet: Sweet peppers are very rich in vitamin C and rich in vitamin A and potassium. Raw sweet peppers contain 8 calories per ounce.

Hot: Hot peppers are 6 times richer in vitamin A than sweet peppers. They are rich in vitamin C and potassium. Each ounce of raw hot peppers contains 12.5 calories.

Recipe for Stuffed Peppers

Stuffed peppers are very popular in Greek and Middle Eastern cuisines. They are easy to prepare. The trick is how to make the rice in the stuffing fluffy.

Ingredients for 4 Servings

1/2 pound ground beef
1 1/2 cups white rice
1 chicken bouillon cube
1/2 cup chopped parsley
1 cup chopped tomatoes
4 big-size or 8 medium-size peppers

Cooking Directions

In a pan, cook the ground beef in 1/2 cup of water until it becomes brown. You don't need to add butter or oil because the ground beef contains fat. Add the rice, chicken bouillon, and 1 1/2 cups water. Cook until the rice absorbs the water. Add the parsley and tomatoes. Stuff the peppers and place them in the pan. Add 1 1/2 cups water and bring to boil. Lower the heat to medium and cook for 20 minutes. Serve hot and enjoy.

Chapter 25

Cucumbers

There is absolutely no comparison between the cucumbers you grow in your garden and those sold in the market. The latter are tough, waxed, and tasteless and the variety is limited. Cucumbers are divided into 2 groups, slicing and pickling. Both can be eaten raw in salad.

Time to Plant Cucumbers

Cucumbers should be planted when the high day temperature exceeds 80° F (26.7° C). In the northern United States and Canada, that would be 2 weeks after the date of last frost. In the South and Pacific West, plant cucumbers in late winter and early spring.

General Information Concerning Cucumbers

There are a few things you should be aware of if you want to grow cucumbers successfully: (1) they are very sensitive to cold weather—a cold spell retards the plants' growth or even kills them; (2) they are sensitive to transplanting; and (3) if their roots are constricted when they are small seedlings, the plants will not grow well, no matter how much water or fertilizers you feed them.

Cucumbers may be grown from seeds sown directly in the garden, seedlings you grow indoors, or seedlings you buy. Seeds are sold in seed catalogs, nurseries, garden centers, and discount stores. The former offer the greatest variety. If you love cucumbers as much as we do, see at least 2 seed catalogs before deciding on what to plant.

The primary considerations when choosing a cucumber variety are taste and disease resistance. When it comes to taste, we highly recommend the *burpless* variety. The fruit grows to 9 to 10 inches long and is eaten whole. Given the right growing conditions, burpless cucumbers are prolific producers. However, the seeds are expensive. You won't find burpless seeds in discount stores. Nurseries and garden centers offer fewer varieties than seed catalogs, and some give small discounts. Discount stores offer 2 or 3 varieties.

Cucumbers can be grown successfully from seedlings bought from nurseries and garden centers. They sell seedlings in packs, each containing 4 to 6 cells with 3 to 4 seedlings in each cell. Many nurseries offer the expensive burpless variety at the same price as other varieties. It is important that you don't buy overgrown seedlings. Check the bottom of the pack to ensure that the roots are not coming out of the drainage holes. Also, don't buy very long seedlings, because their roots may have been constricted in the cells.

Preparing the Soil for Cucumbers

The Conventional Method: Two weeks before transplanting, work some organic material such as peat moss, humus, or dehydrated manure at the rate of 3 pounds per 10 square feet in the top 6 inches of the soil. Next, sprinkle 10-10-10 fertilizer at the rate of one cup per 10 square feet. Water thoroughly.

Theresa's Alternative Method: In the area you allocate for cucumbers, dig 8-inch-deep and 10-inch-across holes 2 feet apart. Prepare potting soil consisting of one part by volume clean topsoil, one part peat moss, and one part dehydrated manure. Add 2 cups 10-10-10 fertilizer to each cubic foot of the potting soil and mix well. Fill the holes with the mix, then water thoroughly.

If you plan to grow cucumbers in containers, replace the dehydrated manure with one part perlite or vermiculite and add one cup bone meal to each cubic foot of the mix.

Planting Cucumbers

If you grow cucumbers from seeds sown directly in the garden, start after the high day temperature exceeds 80° F (26.7° C). In the conventional method, sow 3 or 4 seeds in hills and cover with one inch of soil. The hills should be 2 feet apart in both directions. If you grow from seedlings, empty the contents of the pots or cells in spots spaced 2 feet apart. Firm the soil over the seeds or around the seedlings, then water thoroughly.

In Theresa's alternative method, empty the contents of each pot or cell in each hole that is filled with potting soil. If you grow from seeds sown directly in the ground, sow 3 or 4 seeds in each hole, then cover with one inch of soil. Firm the soil around the seedlings. Water thoroughly.

If you want to grow cucumber seedlings indoors, you should have the proper heating and lighting equipment. If not, the seedlings will grow weak and leggy. Fill 3-inch pots with good potting soil as described above in Theresa's alternative method. Two weeks before the last frost, sow 3 or 4 seeds in each pot. The contents of each pot should be emptied together in the garden in order not to disturb the roots. If you separate the seedlings, the chances are that they will die.

Caring for Cucumbers

Cucumbers should be watered daily and fed monthly with 10-10-10 fertilizer at the rate of 1/4 cup per plant. Don't drop the fertilizer over the leaves or stems to avoid burning them.

Weeds are a problem for cucumbers. Use black plastic sheets as mulch—it keeps the soil warm and conserves water. Watch for diseases and insects. Downy mildew is a big problem for cucumbers. If big brown spots appear on the leaves, take a sample immediately to a big nursery and ask for a cure. The staff will give you a fungicide. Treat the plants without delay, following the manufacturer's instructions. Also, check whether the cucumbers have worms in them.

If big brown spots appear on the leaves, take a sample immediately to a big nursery and ask for a cure.

Harvesting Cucumbers

Cucumbers mature about 6 weeks after transplanting. Like summer squashes, each plant produces male flowers followed by female flowers. Harvest the cucumbers when they reach a reasonable size. Cut them with a knife or twist them in order not to injure the stems. Cucumbers grow fast; therefore, they should be picked every day. Some cucumbers may be hidden under the leaves and will grow very big in a matter of days. If you don't pick them soon, they will form seeds and the plant will stop growing and die.

Cucumber Diseases

Cucumber diseases include powdery mildew, downy mildew, bacterial wilt, mosaic virus, bacterial blight, fusarium wilt, anthracnose, bacterial spot, bacterial rot, leaf spots, and scab.

Cucumber Insects

Cucumber insects include cucumber beetles, squash vine borers, whiteflies, pickleworms, aphids, squash bugs, leafhoppers, and cutworms.

Cucumber Varieties

Slicing: Slicing varieties include Early Spring Burpless, Sweet Success, Tasty Green (resists mildew), Sweet Slice (disease resistant), Fanfare (disease resistant), Spacemaster, Orient Express (disease resistant), Straight Eight, and Marketmore 76 (disease resistant).

Pickling: Pickling varieties include Bush Pickle (disease resistant), Miss Pickler, Pioneer (disease resistant), National Pickling, Carolina (disease resistant), Everbearing, Wisconsin SMR-18, Chicago Pickling (disease resistant), Homemade Pickles (disease resistant), and Bush Baby.

Nutritive Value of Cucumbers

Cucumbers contain potassium, phosphorous, calcium, iron, and vitamins A and C. Most of the vitamins are in the skin. Cucumbers contain only 5 calories per ounce.

Chapter 26

Eggplants

Eggplants are a delicacy in the Mediterranean cuisine. They can be eaten fried or in stews. They also are an essential ingredient in parmigiana, moussaka, and baba ghannouj. The small Italian and white varieties are good for stuffing. Some eggplant recipes are given at the end of this chapter.

Time to Plant Eggplants

Plant eggplants when the high day temperature exceeds 80º F (26.7º C). In cool areas like the northern United States and Canada, that would be 2 weeks after the date of last frost. In areas that don't freeze, like the South or Pacific West, that would be in late winter and early spring.

General Information Concerning Eggplants

Eggplants need full sun. They tolerate drought but should be watered regularly for healthier plants and a bigger harvest. Most eggplants are black, but there are several purple and white varieties. Eggplants are noted for the beauty of their flowers.

Eggplant varieties are divided into bell-shaped, cylindrical, and white. The names of the most widely known varieties of each group are given later in this chapter.

You may grow eggplants from seeds sown directly in the ground, from seedlings you grow indoors, or from seedlings you buy. In areas that freeze in winter, growing eggplants from seeds sown directly in the ground is not practical. In warm areas, it is possible.

The small white variety is good for stuffing.

You may buy eggplant seeds from seed catalogs, nurseries, garden centers, or discount stores. Seed catalogs offer only 2 or 3 varieties. Few offer the white or Italian varieties.

You may buy seedlings from a nearby nursery. They sell packs, each containing 4-6 cells. Buy the seedlings when you are ready to transplant them in the garden. If you keep them for too long in their little cells, the roots will be constricted and the plant's growth retarded.

Preparing the Soil for Eggplants

The Conventional Method: Two weeks before transplanting, work organic matter such as peat moss, humus, or composted manure at the rate of 4 pounds per 10 square feet into the top 6 inches of the soil. Next, sprinkle 5-10-10 fertilizer at the rate of one cup per 10 square feet. Water thoroughly.

Theresa's Alternative Method: In the area you allocate for eggplants, dig 10-inch-wide and 6-inch-deep holes spaced at 2 feet. Prepare potting soil by mixing one part by volume clean topsoil, one part peat moss, and one part composted manure. Add 2 cups 5-10-10 fertilizer to each cubic foot of the potting soil and mix well. Fill the holes with the mix and water thoroughly.

If you plan to grow eggplants in containers, replace the composted manure with one part perlite or vermiculite and add one cup bone meal to each cubic foot of the mix.

Planting Eggplants

In the conventional method, if you grow eggplants from seeds sown directly in the garden, sow one seed every 6 inches and cover with 1/2 inch of soil. When the plants grow to 4 inches high, thin them to 2 feet apart. In Theresa's alternative method, sow 2 seeds in the middle of each hole, then cover with 1/2 inch of soil. When the plants grow to 4 inches high, keep the stronger seedling and pinch or thin the other one.

To grow eggplant seedlings indoors, use heating and lighting equipment.

Sow the seeds 3 weeks before the date of the last frost. Use containers or flats at least 2 inches deep, filled with good potting soil as described above in Theresa's alternative method. Sow the seeds every one inch, 1/2 inch deep. Firm the soil over the seeds, then water thoroughly.

Caring for Eggplants

Cover the area around eggplants with black plastic sheets. Water the eggplants daily, and watch for diseases and insects. Fertilize eggplants every month at the rate of 1/4 cup 5-10-10 fertilizer per plant. If you see a diseased plant, take a sample to a big nursery. The staff will identify the problem and give you a remedy. If you see insects, catch and kill them if they are few. If they are many, take a sample to a nursery. The staff will give you the proper insecticide. Use it according to the manufacturer's directions.

Harvesting Eggplants

Harvest the bulky varieties when they weigh about 3/4 pound, and the slim varieties when they weigh 6 to 8 ounces. At this weight, their taste is sweet. If you let them grow bigger, their taste turns bitter. When harvesting eggplants, cut the stem with a sharp knife.

For best taste, cook the eggplants immediately after harvesting. The surplus can be stored in the refrigerator for a week without losing too much flavor. You may make the surplus into parmigiana or moussaka and freeze it. It can stay frozen for several months without losing flavor.

Eggplant Diseases

Eggplant diseases include verticillium wilt, fusarium wilt, bacterial wilt, leaf spots, downy mildew, powdery mildew, root rot, rust, and anthracnose.

Eggplant Insects

The insects that attack eggplants include flea beetles, aphids, Colorado potato beetles, cutworms, lace bugs, tomato hornworms, and nematodes.

Eggplant Varieties

Bell-shaped: Bell-shaped varieties include Black Beauty, Baby Bell, Black Bell, Dusky, Early Bird, and Blacknite.

Cylindrical: Cylindrical varieties include Neon, Rosita, Vittoria, and Ichiban.

White: White varieties include Casper, Cloud Nine, and Ghostbuster.

Nutritive Value of Eggplants

Eggplants contain potassium, phosphorous, calcium, and vitamins A and C. All varieties contain 7.4 calories per ounce when cooked.

Recipe for Moussaka

Moussaka is a popular Greek and Middle Eastern dish. It is easy to make, tasty, and inexpensive, costing less than 70 cents per serving. The left-overs can be refrigerated or frozen.

Ingredients for 8 Servings

1 1/2 pounds ground beef
2 medium-size onions, chopped
4 cups freshly squeezed tomato juice
1 chicken bouillon cube
4 medium-size eggplants
4 ounces grated cheese
1 teaspoon cinnamon

Cooking Directions

Place the ground beef, chopped onions, tomato juice, and chicken bouillon in a pan. No butter or oil is needed because the ground beef contains fat. Bring to a boil while stirring. Leave on medium heat until the beef is cooked (about 20 minutes).

Meanwhile, slice the eggplants longitudinally into 1/4-inch thick pieces. Fry the eggplants lightly in vegetable oil. Place the slices in a medium-size casserole. Spread the ground beef mix over the eggplants. Sprinkle the grated cheese and cinnamon over the mix. Cover the casserole with aluminum foil and place it in an oven preheated to 400º F (204.4º C). After about 30 minutes remove the aluminum foil. Keep the casserole in the oven until the top takes on the desired brown color. Remove from oven and serve immediately.

Recipe for Baba Ghannouj

Baba ghannouj is a delicacy dip. It is sold in the deli section of supermarkets at a high price. Although its price is steep, it is not as fresh and tasty as the one you make from home-grown eggplants.

Ingredients for 16 Ounces of Baba Ghannouj

1 home-grown eggplant (3/4 pound)
4 ounces sesame tahini
2 tablespoons vegetable oil
Juice of one big lime or lemon
Salt to taste
1/2 teaspoon garlic powder to season (optional)

Cooking Directions

Wash the eggplant, then grill it on the grill or in the oven until it becomes soft all around. After the eggplant cools a little, peel it, cut it in 1-inch cubes, and puree it in the food processor or blender. Empty the puree into a deep dish, add the tahini, vegetable oil, juice of the lime or lemon, and salt. Mix thoroughly. Sprinkle the garlic powder over the top. Serve as needed and refrigerate the rest for future use.

Recipe for Stuffed Eggplants

Ingredients for 8 Servings

8 Italian or slim white eggplants
3/4 pound ground beef
2 cups white rice
1 chicken bouillon cube
1/2 cup chopped parsley
2 medium-sized tomatoes, chopped

Cooking Directions

Cut off the stalk ends of the eggplants, then hollow out the inside with a sharp slim knife or a scoop. Place the ground beef in a pan and cook for 15 minutes. Add the rice, 2 cups of water, and the chicken bouillon. Cook until the rice absorbs the water. Add the parsley and tomatoes and stir for one minute. Stuff the eggplants with the mix.

Place the stuffed eggplants in a pan and add 2 cups of water. Cook for about 25 minutes on medium heat until the rice is done. You know that the meal is cooked when you smell cooked eggplants. Serve hot. Refrigerate or freeze the leftovers.

Chapter 27

Okra

O kra is a delicacy. It is more popular in the South, especially
Louisiana, where it is used in stews and gumbos. Okra grows well
in hot weather and full sun.

Time to Plant Okra

Plant okra when the high day temperature exceeds 85º F (29.4º C). In the
northern United States that would be 3 weeks after the date of last frost. In
the South, that would be early spring. It is very doubtful that okra can be
grown in Canada.

General Information Concerning Okra

Okra is noted for its beautiful hibiscus-like flowers. Okra doesn't transplant well because its roots don't like to be disturbed. Therefore, it should be planted from seeds sown directly in the garden, in containers, or from seedlings grown in individual containers.

The shell of okra seeds is hard. For quicker germination, soak the seeds in warm water for 24 hours before sowing. Seeds may be bought from seed catalogs, nurseries, garden centers, or discount stores. The variety is limited even in seed catalogs. The latter sell packets containing 50 to 100 seeds for a price that varies, depending on the variety. Discount stores sell seed packets for as little as 10 cents a packet. The quality of the seeds is good. However, the number of seeds per packet is much smaller than those offered by seed catalogs.

Growing okra from bought seedlings is not recommended because the roots are likely to be disturbed during transplanting.

Preparing the Soil for Okra

The Conventional Method: Two weeks before transplanting, work organic matter such as peat moss, humus, or composted manure at the rate of 2.5 pounds per 10 square feet into the top 6 inches of the soil. Next, sprinkle 5-10-10 fertilizer at the rate of one cup per 10 square feet. Water thoroughly.

Theresa's Alternative Method: In the area you allocate for okra, dig 6-inch-across and 6-inch-deep holes 1 1/2 feet apart. Prepare potting soil by mixing one part by volume clean topsoil, one part peat moss, and one part composted manure. Add 2 cups 5-10-10 fertilizer to each cubic foot of potting soil and mix well. Fill the holes with the mix and water thoroughly.

If you plan to grow okra in containers, replace the composted manure with one part perlite or vermiculite and add one cup bone meal to each cubic foot of the potting soil.

Planting Okra

To sow okra seeds directly in the garden, the seeds should be covered with 3/4 inch of soil. In the conventional method, sow the seeds every 3 inches in rows 18 inches apart. If you grow from seedlings, transplant a seedling every 1 1/2 feet. Water thoroughly.

In Theresa's alternative method, sow 2 seeds in each hole. When the seedlings reach 3 inches high, cut the weaker seedling and leave the stronger one. If you grow from seedlings grown indoors, empty the contents of each pot in one hole. Water thoroughly.

To grow okra seedlings indoors, use proper heating and lighting equipment. Because seedlings do not transplant well, it is recommended that you grow each seedling in an individual container. Fill the containers with potting soil as explained above in Theresa's alternative method. Sow 2 seeds in each pot. When the plants grow to 2 inches high, leave the stronger and cut the weaker. At the time of transplanting, empty the contents of each pot in a separate spot in the garden. This way, you don't disturb the roots.

Caring for Okra

Cultivate the weeds regularly. Use black plastic sheets as mulch—they keep the soil warm and conserve water. Watch for insects and diseases; pick and destroy any insects you see. Wash away aphids. Don't use chemical pesticides unless the number of insects is great. Also, watch for diseases. If disease becomes a problem, take a sample of the diseased plant to a big nursery. The staff will identify the problem and give you a remedy.

Harvesting Okra

Okra should be picked daily, because the pods grow very fast. It tastes best when picked small, no more than one inch long. The more you pick, the more the plant produces. If not picked small, the pods become huge in a matter of days and the plant stops producing. Okra can be stored in the refrigerator for a few days.

Okra Diseases

Okra diseases include leaf spots, nematodes, root rot, fusarium wilt, powdery mildew, blight, pod rot, and tobacco virus.

Okra Insects

The insects that attack okra include nematodes (nematodes are both diseases and insects), corn earworms, stinkbugs (they produce a foul odor when bothered), aphids, whiteflies, flea beetles, and striped cucumber beetles.

Okra Varieties

Okra varieties include Clemson Spineless, Cajun Delight, Annie Oakley, Dwarf Lee, and Dwarf Long Pod.

Nutritive Value of Okra

Okra is rich in vitamin A. It contains 8 calories per ounce.

Part 6

Herbs

Chapters in This Part

Chapter 28

Parsley

Parsley should not be overlooked by home gardeners because it is full of nutrients, especially vitamins A and C.

Time to Plant Parsley

In cool areas like the northern United States and Canada, parsley should be planted when the weather warms up. This would be mid spring. Although parsley can take light frost, it does not grow well if the weather is cool. In areas that don't freeze, like the South and Pacific West, parsley can be planted in early spring.

General Information Concerning Parsley

Parsley is biennial but should be grown as an annual because a second-year crop grows poorly. It loves full sun but tolerates partial shade.

There are 2 kinds of parsley, Italian (also called plain) and curly. The former is more popular because it has more flavor than the latter. It is used in omelets, soups, and tomato sauces. In Middle Eastern cuisine, Italian parsley replaces lettuce as the main green ingredient in salads. Curly parsley is used to garnish fish and meat dishes. Most people discard it, perhaps thinking that it is not edible.

Parsley may be grown from seeds sown directly in the garden, from seedlings grown indoors, or from bought seedlings. Seeds may be bought from seed catalogs, nurseries, garden centers, or discount stores. Seed catalogs sell Italian parsley packets containing 600 seeds or curly parsley packets containing 150 seeds. Discount stores sell smaller packets for as little as 10 cents.

Parsley seeds take about 20 days to germinate. To reduce germination time, soak the seeds in warm water overnight. Keep the area free of weeds—otherwise, you will get more weeds than parsley!

Growing parsley from bought seedlings is the way we recommend because it saves effort and time. Nurseries and garden centers sell parsley seedlings in packs, each containing 4 to 6 cells, or in trays. Some cells contain individual big seedlings or several small ones. Big seedlings are easier to transplant but more expensive. It is important that you transplant bought seedlings as soon as possible after buying them. Keeping them in small cells causes the roots to be overcrowded and can stunt the growth of the plants.

Preparing the Soil for Parsley

The Conventional Method: Two weeks before transplanting, work organic matter such as peat moss, humus, or dehydrated manure at the rate of 2.5 pounds per 10 square feet into the top 6 inches of the soil. Next, sprinkle 10-10-10 fertilizer at the rate of one cup per 10 square feet. Water thoroughly.

Theresa's Alternative Method: In the area you allocate for parsley, dig 6-inch-deep and 6-inch-across holes 12 inches apart. Prepare potting soil consisting of one part by volume clean topsoil, one part peat moss, and one part dehydrated manure. Add 2 cups 10-10-10 fertilizer to each cubic foot of the potting soil and mix well. Fill the trenches with the mix, then water thoroughly.

If you plan to grow parsley in containers, replace the dehydrated manure with one part perlite or vermiculite and add one cup bone meal to each cubic foot of the mix.

Planting Parsley

Parsley should be transplanted into clean soil that is weed free. If you grow from seeds sown directly in the garden, start 2 weeks after the last frost. If you start earlier, the seeds take very long to germinate.

In the conventional method, sow the seeds 1/2 inch apart and 1/4 inch deep in rows one foot apart. If you grow from seedlings grown indoors or bought, transplant a seedling every 12 inches. In Theresa's alternative method, sow 4 seeds in each hole filled with potting soil and cover with 1/4 inch soil. When the seedlings grow to 3 inches high, leave the strongest seedling and cut or transplant the rest. If you grow from seedlings, transplant one seedling in each hole.

To grow parsley seedlings indoors, it is important to use heating and lighting equipment. Parsley seeds can be grown in any flat or container filled with good potting soil as described in Theresa's alternative method. Sprinkle the seeds 1/2 inch apart and 1/4 inch deep. Firm the soil over the seeds, then water thoroughly.

Parsley seedlings can be grown in any flat or container filled with good potting soil.

Caring for Parsley

Weeds are parsley's biggest enemies. Use either organic mulch or black plastic sheets. Cut holes in them to accommodate the stems. Parsley should be watered regularly and fertilized monthly with 10-10-10 fertilizer at the rate of 1/4 cup per plant. Watch for diseases and insects. If you detect aphids, wash them away with a hose.

Harvesting Parsley

Parsley is harvested when the sprigs are 10 inches high and the leaves are big and thick. Cut the biggest sprigs of each plant 3 inches above the ground. Parsley can be stored in the refrigerator for 1 to 2 weeks. However, for optimum freshness, cut only what you need for immediate consumption.

Parsley plants can stand cold weather but not frost or snow. In the fall, cover the parsley with a clear plastic sheet when the temperature drops below freezing and uncover it when the temperature rises. This way, you can eat fresh parsley from your garden until after Thanksgiving.

In the fall, cover the parsley with a clear plastic sheet when the temperature drops below freezing and uncover it when the temperature rises.

Alternatively, dig up the plants with their roots and attached soil, transplant them into containers, and bring them indoors in a sunny spot. You will eat fresh parsley until after Christmas. Your guests will appreciate eating fresh parsley in the holiday season.

Dig up the parsley plants with their roots and attached soil, transplant them into containers, and bring them indoors.

Parsley Diseases

The diseases that attack parsley include leaf blight, bacterial rot, root rot, leaf spots, and nematodes.

Parsley Insects

The insects that attack parsley include carrot rust flies, cabbage loopers, celeryworms, spider mites, and aphids.

Parsley Varieties

The 2 basic parsley varieties are the Italian (plain) and the curly.

Nutritive Value of Parsley

Parsley is very rich in vitamins A, B, and C, iron, calcium, and phosphorous. It contains 14 calories per ounce.

Medicinal Value of Parsley

According to *Prescription for Nutritional Healing,* by James F. Balch and Phyllis A. Balch, parsley contains a substance that prevents multiplication of tumor cells, refreshens breath, and helps the bladder, kidney, liver, lung, stomach, and thyroid functions.

Chapter 29

Mint

Mint is a fragrant herb. Its leaves can be made into teas or mixed with ordinary teas to add flavor. Mint is also used to flavor stews, salads, and sauces.

Time to Plant Mint

Because mint is a perennial, it can be planted at any time of the season. It takes winter frost and snow and comes back the following spring.

General Information Concerning Mint

Mint becomes dormant during winter. The following spring, numerous new seedlings emerge all over the surrounding area. Controlling mint can be a problem. Early in the season, cover the area you don't want mint to grow in with black plastic mulch.

There are several varieties of mint—the best known are spearmint and peppermint. The latter is spicier and its leaves smaller and darker than the former.

Mint can be grown in a wide variety of soils. The easiest way to grow mint is to buy a pot containing seedlings from a nursery or garden center and transplant it into the ground. A less expensive way to grow mint is to dig up some seedlings from a friend's garden with as much soil as possible attached to their roots. Your friend loses nothing because more mint will grow and replace those you have taken.

A less expensive way to grow mint is to dig up some seedlings from a friend's garden with as much soil as possible attached to their roots.

Planting Mint

Mint doesn't require special soil. Of course, it grows better if the soil is fertile. To plant mint, dig a hole 8 inches wide and 6 inches deep in a sunny location. Add a shovel of peat moss mixed with composted manure to the dug-up soil and mix them well. Empty the pot containing mint seedlings (or the seedlings you dug up from your friend's garden) into the middle of the hole. Fill around the seedlings with the soil mixture, then firm the soil around the plant. Water thoroughly.

Caring for Mint

Mint needs little care. It grows and spreads year after year with little or no effort on your part. However, mint should be watered regularly and fertilized twice a year with 10-10-10 fertilizer at the rate of one cup per 10 square feet. If you don't feed mint, it becomes susceptible to diseases.

Weeds may take over mint. Therefore, you should cultivate the weeds while they are small. Watch for diseases. Once mint is infected, the disease spreads quickly to the rest of the plants. The solution is to cut all infected plants and discard them safely. A new healthy crop will grow in their place in a few weeks.

Harvesting Mint

Harvest mint when the sprigs reach 6 inches high. Mint is fresher and more fragrant early in the season. As the season progresses and the plants grow taller, cut them about 6 inches above ground. The more you harvest mint, the more it grows and spreads. At the end of the season, harvest the entire crop and dry or freeze it.

Mint Diseases

Mint diseases include leaf spots, powdery mildew, verticillium wilt, fusarium wilt, and nematodes.

Mint Insects

The insects that attack mint include mint flea beetles, mealybugs, weevils, and aphids.

Mint Varieties

Mint varieties include Peppermint, Spearmint, Apple, Pineapple, Orange, and Chocolate.

Medicinal Value of Mint

Mint is good for digestion and for fighting cold, diarrhea, headache, and poor appetite. However, it is acidic, which means you shouldn't use it if you have acidic stomach.

Chapter 30

Basil

Basil includes several varieties, the most popular of which is sweet basil. It is widely used to season Italian tomato sauces, grilled chicken, meat, and fish.

Time to Plant Basil

Basil is an annual herb. It doesn't tolerate frost. It should be planted when the high day temperature exceeds 70º F (21.1º C). In cool areas like the northern United States and Canada, this would be mid to late spring. In areas that don't freeze, like the South and Pacific West, it could be planted in early spring.

General Information Concerning Basil

Basil needs light soil that is high in organic matter. It grows best in full sun but tolerates partial shade. It can be grown in containers outdoors or indoors in a sunny spot.

You may grow basil from seeds sown directly in the garden, from seedlings grown indoors, or from seedlings you buy. Seed catalogs sell basil packets each containing 50 to 150 seeds. You may also buy basil seeds from nurseries, garden centers, or discount stores. Another source is to dry the seeds the plants produce at the end of the season.

In cool areas, it is better to grow basil from seedlings bought from nurseries and garden centers. They sell packs, each containing 4 to 6 cells. In warm areas, sow the seeds directly in the ground in early spring.

It is important that you transplant basil seedlings shortly after you buy them. If you let them stay in their cells for too long, the roots will be constricted and the plants will grow weak.

Preparing the Soil for Basil

The Conventional Method: Two weeks before transplanting, work organic matter such as peat moss, humus, or dehydrated manure at the rate of one pound per 4 square feet into the top 6 inches of the soil. Next, apply 10-10-10 fertilizer at the rate of one cup per 10 square feet. Water thoroughly.

Theresa's Alternative Method: In the area you allocate for basil, dig 8-inch-deep and 8-inch-wide holes 12 inches apart. Prepare potting soil by mixing one part by volume clean topsoil, one part peat moss, and one part dehydrated manure. Add one cup 10-10-10 fertilizer to each cubic foot of the mix. Fill the holes with the mix and water thoroughly.

If you plan to grow basil in containers, replace the dehydrated manure with one part perlite or vermiculite and add one cup bone meal to each cubic foot of the mix.

Planting Basil

In the conventional method, plant basil in rows 12 inches apart. Sow the seeds 2 inches apart and 1/2 inch deep. As they grow, thin them to 12 inches apart. If you grow from seedlings, transplant one seedling every 12 inches.

In Theresa's alternative method, sow 4 seeds in each hole. When they grow to one inch high, keep the strongest seedling and cut the rest. If you grow from seedlings, transplant one seedling in each hole.

If the weather doesn't allow the transplant of bought seedlings in the ground shortly after you buy them, transplant them into bigger containers until the weather warms up. This gives the roots room to grow and expand. Water thoroughly.

If you want to grow seedlings indoors, start 4 weeks before the date of last frost. Use flats 2 inches deep or 3-inch pots. Fill them with good potting soil as explained above in Theresa's alternative method. For healthy seedlings, use the proper heating and lighting equipment.

Caring for Basil

It is important to cultivate the weeds regularly. Use organic mulch or black plastic sheets. The latter is recommended. Fertilize basil lightly in order to preserve its strong aroma. If you give the basil too much water and fertilizer, the plants grow big, but their aroma diminishes. Use 10-10-10 fertilizer at the rate of one tablespoon per plant per month. Water regularly.

Pinch the basil flowers as soon as they form; otherwise the plants will form seeds and die.

Harvesting Basil

Start harvesting basil when the plants grow big and bushy. Cut leaves or little branches with the leaves on. Basil may be frozen for future use.

Basil Diseases

The most common basil disease is root knot nematodes.

Basil Insects

Basil has no insect problem.

Basil Varieties

Basil varieties include Sweet, Lemon, Anise, Cinnamon, Purple Ruffles, Thai Siam Queen, Spicy Globe, and Large-Leafed Italian.

Chapter 31

Catnip

C atnip is a hardy perennial. It withstands frost and snow and comes back very early the following season. Cats love catnip for reasons only cats know!

General Information Concerning Catnip

Catnip grows well in light soil. It withstands thirst. Unless you live in an arid area, rain provides catnip with the water it needs to grow. Catnip grows so fast that you will have enough of it no matter how much you cut it.

Cats love catnip. Sometimes, we entertain our guests by bringing a catnip leaf to our cat Alley. After sniffing and biting the leaf for a few seconds, she rolls over and over in ecstacy while we watch in amazement. However, we are careful not to expose Alley to catnip more than once a year for fear that it may be addictive to her.

Some people claim that catnip is good for fighting hysteria! Although neither of us suffers from hysteria, we tried catnip tea a couple of times, just out of curiosity. Unfortunately, we didn't feel any improvement in our psychological behavior!

Sometimes, we entertain our guests by bringing a catnip leaf to our cat Alley. After sniffing and biting the leaf for a few seconds, she rolls over and over in ecstacy while we watch in amazement, as shown in this and the following 3 photos.

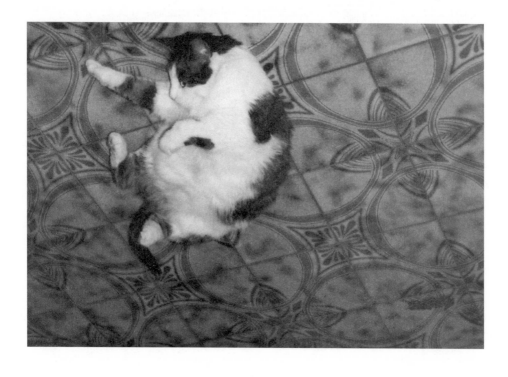

Planting Catnip

The easiest way to grow catnip is to buy a seedling from a nursery or garden center. Dig a hole 8 inches wide and 8 inches deep. Mix the dug-up soil with a shovel of peat moss. Empty the pot containing the catnip seedling into the hole, then fill around it with the dug-up soil. Water thoroughly.

Caring for Catnip

To keep catnip healthy, fertilize once a year with 10-10-10 fertilizer at the rate of one tablespoon per plant. In the fall, catnip produces seeds which are carried long distances by the wind. Early next season, you will find catnip seedlings emerging everywhere.

Catnip Diseases

Catnip diseases include bacterial leaf spots, blight, root rot, mosaic virus, and fusarium wilt.

Catnip Insects

The insects that attack catnip include leafhoppers and webworms.

Catnip Varieties

There are no catnip varieties.

Medicinal Value of Catnip

According to Rodale's *Illustrated Encyclopedia of Herbs:*

> A tea made from the dried leaves and flowering heads (of catnip) has been used to treat just about everything from colds to cancer.

Index

Index

Index